Primary Sources of World Cultures

INDIA

A PRIMARY SOURCE CULTURAL GUIDE

Allison Stark Draper

The Rosen Publishing Group's
PowerPlus Books™
New York

For my mother

Published in 2003 by The Rosen Publishing Group, Inc.
29 East 21st Street, New York, NY 10010

Library of Congress Cataloging-in-Publication Data

Draper, Allison Stark.
India: a primary source cultural guide / Allison Stark Draper.— 1st ed.
   p. cm. — (Primary sources of world cultures)
Summary: An overview of the history and culture of India and its people including the geography, myths, arts, daily life, education, industry, and government, with illustrations from primary source documents.
Includes bibliographical references and index.
ISBN 0-8239-3838-7 (library binding)
1. India—Juvenile literature. [1. India.] I. Title. II. Series.
DS407 .D73 2003
954—dc21

                                                              2002015437

Manufactured in the United States of America

Cover Images: Text from the Mahabharata (background script); Victoria Memorial in Calcutta; Proud Rajput man

Photo credits: Cover images © Lindsay Hebberd/Corbis, Jean-Louis Nou/AKG London, Photri; pp. 3, 118 © ILLUSTRATOR MAP; p. 4 (top) © Viesti Associates, Inc./Dinodia; p. 4 (middle) © Angelo Homak/Corbis; p. 4 (bottom) © Suraj N. Sharma/Images of India Picture Agency; p. 5 (top) © DPA/The Image Works; p. 5 (middle) © Ian Cumming/Axiom; p. 5 (bottom) © Images of India Picture Agency; pp. 6, 8, 38, 96, 118 (top inset), 120 © Ian Cumming/Axiom/ Corbis; pp. 7, 10, 99, 102 © Chris Caldicott/Axiom; p. 9 © National Geographic; pp. 11, 54, 58, 68, 85 © Lindsay Hebberd/Woodfin Camp & Associates; p. 12 © Viesti Associates, Inc./Dinodia; p. 13 © Paolo Koch/Photo Researchers Inc.; p. 14 © Photri-Microstock; pp. 15, 16 (bottom), 17, 22 (bottom), 33, 34, 37, 41 (bottom), 47, 90 (top), 95 (bottom), 97 (top and bottom), 98, 100, 101 (top and bottom), 103, 107 (top and bottom), 117 (left) © Dinodia; pp. 18, 117 (right) © Paul Almasy/Corbis; p. 19 © Ric Ergenbright/ Corbis; pp. 20, 30 (bottom) © Corbis; pp. 21, 43, 62 © Scala/Art Resource NY; p. 22 (top) © Dagli Orti/Epigraphical Museum, Athens/Art Archive; p. 23 © Charles & Josette Lenars/Corbis; pp. 24, 118 (bottom right) © Chris Lisle/Corbis; p. 26 © Stapleton Collection/Corbis; pp. 27, 64, 76 (bottom), 81 © Victoria & Albert Museum, London/Art Resource; p. 28 © Granger Collection; p. 29 © Bettmann/Corbis; p. 30 (top) © Hulton-Deutsch Collection/Corbis; p. 31 © Hulton-Deutsch Collection/Corbis; pp. 32 (top), 77, 88 © Hulton/Archive by Getty Images; p. 32 (bottom) © Underwood & Underwood/ Corbis; p. 35, 44 © Dinodia Picture Agency; p. 36 by Tahara Hasan; p. 39 © Chandra Kishore Prasad/Link Picture Library; pp. 40, 57 (bottom), 106 (top), 106 (bottom), 109 © Axiom; p. 41 (top) © Joe Viesti/Viesti Associates, Inc.; p. 42 © Ned Gillette/Image State; pp. 46, 84 © Freer Gallery of Art/The Smithsonian Institution; p. 48 © Mary Evans Picture Library; p. 49 © Angelo Homak/Corbis; pp. 51, 60, 110 © Reuters NewMedia Inc./Corbis; pp. 52, 56 © AFP/Corbis; p. 53 © Chris Lisle/Corbis; p. 55 © Ralph Davis/Aurora Photos; p. 57 (top) © Suraj N. Sharma/Images of India Picture Agency; p. 59 © The Image Works, Inc.; pp. 61, 91 (top and bottom), 92 © Lindsay Hebberd/Corbis; p. 63 © Government of India Tourist Office NY; p. 65 © Paul Quayle/Axiom; p. 66 © David Samuel Robbins/Corbis; p. 67 © Macduff Everton/ImageState; p. 69 © Jeroen Snijders/Images of India Picture Agency; p. 70 © Hideo Haga/The Image Works; pp. 71, 94 © Joe Beynon/Axiom; p. 73 © Sean Sprague/The Image Works; p. 74 © David Wells/The Image Works; p. 75 © Borromeo/Art Resource; p. 76 (top) © Jean-Louis Nou/AKG London; p. 78 © Macduff Everton/Corbis; p. 79 © SEF/Art Resource; p. 80 © A. Ramey/Woodfin Camp & Associates; p. 82 © FMDPA Images of India/Link Picture Agency; p. 83 (top) © Vicki Couchman/Axiom; p. 83 (bottom) © S. Nagendra/Photo Researchers, Inc.; p. 86 © Merrill Images/International Stock; p. 87 © Image State; p. 89 © VDA-DPA/The Image Works; p. 90 (bottom) © Barnabas Bosshart/Corbis; p. 93 © Luca Tettoni/The Viesti Collection; p. 95 © Gharp; p. 104 © Images of India Picture Agency; p. 105 © Paul Quayle; Images of India Picture Agency; p. 108 © Jayesh Mehta/Dinodia Picture Agency; p. 112 © Bettmann/Corbis; p. 118 (bottom left) © Roman Soumar/Corbis; p. 121 © Karen Su/Corbis.

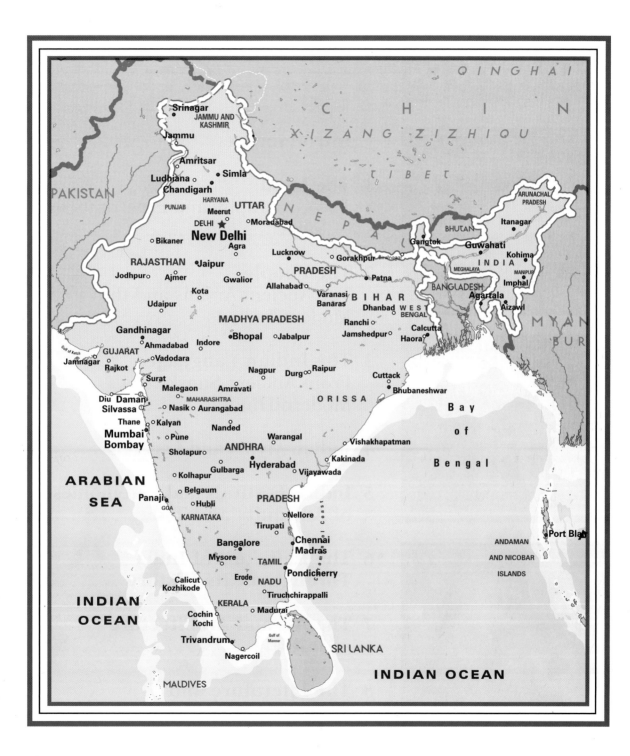

CONTENTS

Introduction 7

1 **The Land**
The Geography and Environment
of India 11

2 **The People**
The Ancient Aryans and the
Modern Indians 19

3 **The Indian Languages**
From Ancient Sanskrit to
Modern Hindi 39

4 **Indian Myths and Legends** 47

5 **Indian Festivals and Ceremonies
of Antiquity and Today** 53

6 **The Religions of India
Throughout Its History** 63

7 **The Art and Architecture
of India** 75

8 **The Literature and
Music of India** 85

9 Famous Foods and Recipes of India 93

10 Daily Life and Customs in India 99

11 Education and Work in India . .105

India at a Glance 112

    History 112
    Economy 113
    Government and Politics 114
    Timeline 116
    Map .118
    Fact Sheets 119

Glossary 122

For More Information 123

For Further Reading 123

Bibliography 124

Primary Source Image List 124

Index 126

INTRODUCTION

India is an immense and ancient country. It stretches from the snow-glazed Himalayas to the steamy southern tip of Tamil Nadu. In between lie deserts, forests, palm-lined beaches, and endless acres of farmland. India is also a land dotted with magnificent palaces and delicate temples. These are the legacy of 4,000 years of lavish emperors and gifted architects. Today, India is a modern nation and a leader in world industry. Its population is as vast and various as its history. The country's one billion people share more than a dozen religions and speak more than a thousand languages.

The rich diversity of Indian culture comes from its willingness to absorb new ideas. India's first known civilization, the Indus River Valley culture, fell to Aryan conquerors in 1500 BC. The Aryans' beliefs merged with native Indian ideas. This blend of civilizations created India's Hindu culture. One thousand years later, Indian Buddhists adopted the styles of Greek sculptors who entered India with Alexander the Great.

The city of Delhi dates back to 1400 BC. It was referred to as the settlement of Indraprastha in the ancient Hindu epic the Mahabharata. Delhi has seen many rulers, and it became a Mughal capital in 1526. The Jama Masjid (Mosque) in Delhi *(left)* was once the largest in India. It expressed the grandeur of the flourishing Muslim culture of the period. This spectacular view to the north *(above)*, a photograph taken from the Indian state of Himachal Pradesh, shows the Himalayas in the background.

The Taj Mahal, located in Agra, India, is considered one of the most magnificent architectural wonders of the world. This Islamic tomb was built by Emperor Shah Jahan to memorialize his wife, Mumtaz Mahal, who died during the birth of their fourteenth child. Completed in 1648, the Taj Mahal was constructed of white marble and red sandstone, and decorated with gold, silver, turquoise, rubies, and other precious and semiprecious stones.

The Muslim invaders of the tenth century AD built smooth geometric mosques in northern India. These were radically different from the densely carved temples of southern India. Over time, aspects of the two styles merged. The native Indian love of nature added lifelike flowers and animals to the cool elegance of Muslim art.

In the eighteenth century, India fell to British rule. The British helped modernize India, building railroads and telegraph systems. England's legal and judicial systems became the basis for modern Indian government. Indians who spoke different dialects used English as a common language.

In the twentieth century, Indians grew dissatisfied with British colonialism. The national movement for independence from the British intensified under the leadership of Mohandas Karamchand Gandhi. In 1947, India won its independence from Great Britain. It freed itself from British leadership but kept the ideas that were useful to it. For example,

modern Indian universities still follow British education models. English continues to help people from different regions communicate with one another.

India has been an independent nation for more than half a century, making enormous advances in industry and agriculture. With more than a billion people, it is the largest democracy in the world. In fact, half of all the people in the world who live in a democratic society currently reside in India.

Modern culture is global culture. Advances in transportation and telecommunications link every country in the world in a global net. Given its ancient tradition of taking the best ideas from the countries it encounters, India is perfectly poised to be a leader in the twenty-first century.

India embraces both ancient and modern customs, as illustrated in this crowded scene of bicycles, camels, and cars competing for space in the city of Jaipur. Located in the northwestern province of Rajasthan, Jaipur shares a border with Pakistan along the Thar Desert. The intense, dry heat of the region explains why camels are a popular method of transportation here.

THE LAND

The Geography and Environment of India

I ndia, the world's seventh largest country, is a subcontinent bounded by mountains in the north and the Indian Ocean in the south. Its neighboring lands are Nepal and China in the north; Pakistan in the northwest; and Myanmar (Burma), Bhutan, and Bangladesh in the east. India is divided into three geographical areas: the mountain region, the fertile plains, and the southern coast. The Himalayan mountains mark the country's northern edge. The Indo-Gangetic Plain runs across the middle, from Pakistan's Indus River to the Ganges River, which runs through India and empties into eastern Bangladesh. The pointed southern peninsula creates the 4,375-mile (7,000 km) coastline that has protected India from invasion and made it an ancient trading capital. Peninsular India lies on one of the world's oldest landmasses, and its three regions lie almost entirely on one tectonic plate. For the past 130 million years, this plate's collision with the Central Asian plate has been forcing up the Himalayas.

Much of the Indian peninsula is made of Archean rocks, which are the oldest rocks in the world. Belts of this ancient rock stripe the Nilgiri and Palani Hills, the Eastern Ghats, Rajasthan, and the Aravalli-Delhi belt. They yield valuable manganese, iron, and marble, and are home to India's gold mines. Sedimentary formations in the Vindhya Mountains have produced the famous Panna and Golconda diamonds.

The Indo-Gangetic Plain formed about 40 million years ago, when the peninsula merged with Asia. As it moved north, it slid under the Himalayan edge of the Asian plate. This created a low area that floods with excess water from the Indus and Ganges Rivers, creating rich farmland.

Palm trees, commonly found on the Indian island of Goa *(left)*, were among the first flora sighted by the European explorer Vasco da Gama, who later used the island as a sixteenth-century Portuguese port. The western Himalayan mountain range *(above)* runs through India's Himachal Province. Its wide range of elevation produces various climates in the region, from subhumid tropics in the southern lowlands to glacial conditions in the northern and eastern high mountains. The snow-fed waters of the Chenab, Ravi, Beas, Sutlej, and Yamuna Rivers flow through Himachal Province and feed into the Indus and Ganges basins farther south.

These rice terraces—an example of agricultural engineering—are located in the northern town of Leh, Ladakh. Mountain slopes are transformed into steps and utilize the gravity of downward flowing streams to provide water to rice crops. Nearly 65 percent of India's populace depends on rice as a staple food.

The youngest section of India is the Himalayan mountain range, home to Mount Everest. The Himalayas run northwest to southeast for approximately 1,600 miles (2,500 km).

The Climate

Because of its large size, India has various microclimates that vary radically in humidity and temperature. Rajasthan is a desert, while India's northern Shillong Plateau is among the wettest places in the world. The Himalayas rise so abruptly that within a few miles, the temperature shifts from semitropical to arctic.

Throughout most of the country, however, May is the hottest month and January is the coldest. The winter season in India is mostly dry, while summer and autumn are typically marked by rainy weather. India's seasons follow the monsoon winds. Twice a year, the direction of the wind rotates at least 120 degrees. When the summer sun grows hotter, the temperature of the land and ocean rises because they absorb heat. On land, the heat bounces back up into the atmosphere, which,

in turn, changes wind pressure and wind patterns. The western wind that blows across the Indo-Gangetic Plain during winter swings to the east. Dry western air suddenly changes to wet southwesterly winds from the Maldives and Sri Lanka. These winds blow across India into Pakistan, bringing with them violent, drenching rainstorms.

India's winter monsoon season occurs between October and December. Dry, cold high-pressure systems build over Central Asia, north of the Himalayas. These polar patterns replace the western winds with chilly northeasterly winds. But because India is protected by the Himalayas, its winter monsoon season is mild.

The streets of Benares turn into virtual rivers during the monsoon season. One of the most severe weather occurrences on Earth, monsoons are caused by a reversal in wind direction along the shores of the Indian Ocean. The summer, or southwest, monsoon season begins in mid-June and can last until early October. Seventy-five percent of India's annual rainfall occurs during the summer monsoon season.

The Environment

People have been farming in India for thousands of years. To open the land for farms, they have cut down millions of square miles of forest. In its natural state,

At times worth more than its weight in gold, saffron, a spice introduced to India by the Mongols nearly 2,000 years ago, is cultivated as a cash crop in Kashmir. A perennial of the iris family, saffron is prized for its golden colored stigmas, which are used to flavor food and dye cloth. The stigmas are hand-picked, laid on trays, and dried over charcoal fires.

most of India would be forested. Today, 55 percent of the land is cultivated. Only 250,000 square miles (400,000 square kilometers) of forest remain in a country of almost 2.5 million square miles (4 million square kilometers).

India's largest forest type was once the tropical deciduous forest that covered most of its northwestern territory. To clear this land for agriculture, farmers burned existing vegetation. This method turned the fire-resistant sal and teak trees into India's most common species. The wood of both is valuable for building. Other trees have suffered more drastically. Rosewood, which is used to create furniture, and sandalwood, which is scented, are both extremely rare.

There are still long stretches of tropical evergreen forest along the ridges of the Western Ghats. Coconut palms grow on the west coast and, along with palmyra, are common in the south and east. The wet hill forests of the Himalayas are too steep

Although India is a vastly populated country, eastern India still harbors some of the world's unspoiled primeval forests, rich in wildlife and untapped resources. Indian environmentalists, some of them part of the Chipko movement, often protect trees from being felled by sitting in them for extended periods. "Chipko" literally means "to embrace."

The Indian cobra, or *Naja naja*, lurks mainly in the tropical forests and grasslands of India and appears as an important character in Hindu mythology. When threatened, it will expand its flexible neck ribs to form a distinctive hood. It feasts on a diet of rodents, lizards, and frogs, stunning its prey with a quick, venom-laced bite.

for farming, and most remain full of evergreen oaks and chestnuts. Pines, cedars, firs, and spruces are also plentiful. In parts of the foothills, these forests end at the savannah grasslands that fringe the dense bamboo region of the eastern Himalayas.

The soil that supports most of India's farms and forests is the red soil of ancient Archean rocks. It is light, workable soil, but it does not hold moisture well. The peninsula's other major soil is a black volcanic clay. It is rich and wet but difficult to drain. Overall, India's climate supports a variety of vegetation.

Wildlife

India is home to a wonderful variety of animal species. More than 350 types of mammals flourish on the subcontinent. There are 900 different reptiles and amphibians, 2,000 kinds of birds, and 30,000 types of butterflies and insects. Almost any of the world's animals could find a suitable climate in India. There are otters in the Himalayas and dolphins in the mouths of the Indus and Ganges Rivers. The

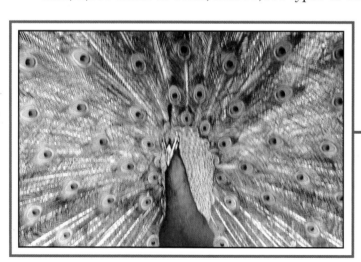

The peacock is the national bird of India. Here we see the male peacock spreading its plumage to reveal a spectacle of color. Why all this showmanship? Males strut their stuff in order to attract a female peahen, which selects her male partners based upon their number of eyespots, or ocelli.

Although tigers have been hunted nearly to extinction in India, programs such as Project Tiger, begun in 1973, have helped to stabilize India's endangered tiger population. In some areas, the teak forests and terai grass that are the tigers' native habitat have been largely protected from development and are off-limits to poachers as a result of the initiative.

Indian mongoose, valiant foe of the deadly cobra, lives all over the country. The king cobra, largest of the world's poisonous snakes, tends to favor forests, as do most of India's martens, weasels, ferrets, badgers, shrews, hedgehogs, moles, bats, squirrels, and anteaters. Indian birds include the splendid eagles and falcons of the north; the ducks, cranes, and swallows that migrate annually from central Asia; vivid parakeets, woodpeckers, and kingfishers; and the gorgeous national bird, the peacock.

Larger species, like elephants, rhinoceroses, lions, and wild bears have fallen prey to poachers or have lost their homes to deforestation. There are now only about 15,000 elephants in India. Sixty-five hundred live in the northeast and over the border in Bhutan. There are 2,000 in central India and 6,000 in the south. There are only 1,500 one-horned rhinos in northern India, in the states of Assam and West Bengal, and Nepal.

Hunting, poaching, and deforestation have hurt India's big cat populations, decimating its lions and eliminating its cheetahs. A few snow leopards still lope through the high Himalayas. The black panther, though rare, covers much of its original territory. India's most famous big cat, the spectacular Bengal tiger, once prowled the forests in the tens of thousands. Now, roughly 4,000 live on protected nature preserves.

Indian environmentalism is ancient. Two thousand years ago, the Buddhist emperor Asoka outlawed the killing of wildlife. He declared forests *abhayaranya*, or "free of fear." Modern India has 20 major wildlife sanctuaries, 121 national parks, and 9 bird reserves. Altogether, they cover 35,000 square miles (90,000 square kilometers).

THE PEOPLE

2

The Ancient Aryans and the Modern Indians

The northernmost part of India is the state of Jammu and Kashmir, an area claimed by both India and Pakistan. Below this is Punjab, or the "Land of the Five Rivers." The westernmost waterway is the Indus River, which runs through the Indus River Valley. In 1856, at a work site near the Indus village of Harappa, railway workers made a major archaeological discovery. They dug up small squares of carved soapstone, tiles that became the first evidence of the earliest known Indian civilization.

Sixty years later, another archaeological team excavated a site now known as Mohenjo-Daro ("Mound of the Dead"), 400 miles (644 kilometers) southeast of Harappa. Perfectly preserved, Mohenjo-Daro provided certain evidence of the sophisticated urban civilization that thrived in the Indus River Valley in 2000 BC. Both cities had housed 35,000 people in tidy grids of houses, shops, and temples, complete with drainage systems. Massive citadels towered more than fifty feet (fifteen meters) each.

Before the discovery at Harappa, Indian history was believed to date back to the Vedic texts of 1500 BC. These Vedas, or Books of Knowledge, describe the invasion of India by the Aryan followers of the god Indra, the "Hurler of the

The word "Hindu" is derived from the Sanskrit word for river, *sindhu*. This section of the Indus River *(above)* flows through the disputed Indian territory of Jammu and Kashmir. The ancient city of Mohenjo-Daro *(left)* blossomed on the Indus River around 2000 BC. Its citizens stored surplus food in a granary, bathed in ritual baths, and had at least two assembly halls. The Harappan civilization eventually declined when the Indus River changed its course about 3,700 years ago. It is located in what is now southern Pakistan.

Thought to be of a priest figure, this sculpture offers clues about the religious beliefs that existed at Mohenjo-Daro. It is now on display at the Karachi Museum in Pakistan. Although the names of their gods are unknown and their language is still undeciphered, it is thought that a king who was worshiped like a god ruled the Harappan civilization.

Thunderbolt." The Aryans defeated a dark-skinned, urban people they called Dasas, who may have been the Harappans. After their victory, the Aryans thanked Indra for destroying the Dasas' citadels "as age consumes a garment."

The devastation of the Dasas was only partly due to Aryan military strength. Over time, the geological plate beneath the mouth of the Indus River had lifted and slowed the river flow. Blocked water spread back across the lowlands and flooded Mohenjo-Daro, 200 miles (320 kilometers) inland. By the time the Aryans appeared in their horse-drawn chariots, wielding weapons of bronze, the Indus River Valley civilization was in decline.

The Vedic Age

The Aryan nomads, possibly traveling from Persia (Iran) around 1500 BC, settled in northern India and blended their cattle-herding skills with local farming practices. They became known as Hindus, from the word "Indus." Their Vedic priests—men who studied the Vedas—introduced the caste system. The Aryan (Sanskrit) word for caste was *varna*, which means "color."

The caste system divided society into Brahmins, Kshatriyas, Vaishyas, and Shudras. The Brahmins were priests; they performed religious rituals and communicated with the gods. Kshatriyas were rulers and warriors. Vaishyas were merchants who handled money and trade. Shudras performed menial labor and worked the earth as farmers. Each group was crucial to society. Outside this system were outcastes, or "untouchables." They were considered polluted. Outcastes performed "unclean" tasks, like handling dead bodies and garbage. Over time, the Vedic caste system became impossibly rigid. By the sixth century BC, religions that did not follow the caste system, like Buddhism, founded by Siddhartha Gautama, and Jainism, founded by

This sculpture, originally from Gunbat and now housed in the Museo Nazionale d'Arte Orientale in Rome, Italy, shows Brahma and Indra inviting the Buddha to preach. It was made in the first or second century AD in the Gandhara style, which is considered the height of Buddhist expression. It showcases the merging of Greco-Roman ideals and Indian Buddhist beliefs.

Vardhamana Mahavira, were gaining converts.

In the fourth century BC, the Nanda dynasty took control of the Ganges Valley. They built a kingdom based on military power. Peoples as far west as the Persians and Greeks knew of the might of the Nandas. In 530 BC, the Persian king, Cyrus, invaded and conquered northwestern Gandhara. Two hundred years later, in 327 BC, Alexander the Great led the Greeks through Persia and into India, bringing Greek ideas into Indian culture. When the Greeks faltered, Chandragupta Maurya seized power. In 321 BC, he began the Mauryan Empire.

The Mauryas reigned from 321 to 185 BC and developed India's first true empire. Chandragupta I kept an army of half a million soldiers. In 305 BC, he took the Indus River region back from the Greeks. His successor, Bindusara, stretched the border south to Mysore. The next emperor, Asoka, conquered eastern Kalinga (modern-day Orissa). India was now divided into separate states, each with its own ruler. Horrified by the devastation of war, Asoka turned to the peaceful religion of Buddhism. Convinced that a king should protect his subjects, he built roads, rest houses, and hospitals. In an early form of mass communication, Asoka carved edicts (laws) onto stone posts and erected them across his vast empire from Mysore to what is now Afghanistan. Asoka's embrace of Buddhism helped the religion spread farther, becoming well-known as far away as central and southeast Asia. Buddhism is still practiced in India today. India's national monument is one of the remaining

This Roman mosaic shows Alexander the Great, king of Macedonia, at the Battle of Issus in 333 BC. Alexander the Great invaded India by way of Persia in 327 BC. He is credited with introducing Greek culture, or Hellenism, to the Indian subcontinent.

pillars of Asoka, an artistic symbol of spiritual enlightenment.

When the Mauryan Empire declined, a group of Brahmin officials took power. They were succeeded by the Bactrian Greeks, the Scythians, the Parthians, and then, in the first century AD, the central Asian Kushanas. The Kushanas became Buddhists and spread Buddhism north to China.

The Golden Age

By AD 319, the Indian Guptas wiped out the Kushanas and began what has sometimes been called the Indian Golden or Classical Age—more than 200 years of peace and creativity. Under Chandragupta II, Indian kingdoms were consolidated into a larger empire that began a great cultural renaissance. Leaders encouraged the study of mathematics, astronomy, medicine, law, literature, and the arts. Detailed Buddhist frescoes inside the Ajanta Caves celebrated this

This photograph, which shows prehistoric paintings located inside a cave in Bhopal, India, dates from the Neolithic, or New Stone Age (4000–2500 BC), a period before the settlements of Mohenjo-Daro and Harappa. Cave painting in India was practiced for thousands of years, reaching its height during the sixth century AD.

growth of creativity. The Buddhist sculpture and dramatic feats of Hindu architecture of that time provide modern scholars with a record of daily life. India's Golden Age also spawned the mathematician and astronomer Aryabhata, who provided India with accurate theories about the rotation of the earth on its axis. He calculated the length of a year as 365 days. Literature and poetry experienced tremendous growth at this time, including, but not limited to, religious verse. The well-known poet and dramatist Kalidasa, often compared to Shakespeare, was one of the "nine gems" of the court of Chandragupta II.

The Ajanta cave paintings were created during the sixth century AD and typify the exquisite art produced during the Golden Age of the Gupta dynasty. This scene shows the lavish court life of Prince Gautama before he forsakes his worldly comforts to learn about the life of poverty beyond the palace walls. It is only then that he reaches enlightenment and becomes the Buddha.

Southern India

The constant political drama of the north had little effect on the far south. Southern India was divided into three Tamil-speaking kingdoms; Tamil is now the oldest living language in the world. The Cholas held the east coast near what is now Chennai (Madras). The Cheras of Kerala ruled the west. The Pandyas controlled the center to the

tip of Tamil Nadu. The Pandya capital of Madurai was a meeting place of poets, philosophers, and artists. Today, it remains a magnificent city of temples.

Tamil society was based on geography, rather than on northern India's caste system. There were hill people, plains people, forest people, coastal people, and desert people. These divisions were composed of smaller groups of people and were often based upon the work they accomplished. For example, coastal peoples included pearl divers, sailors, and boat builders.

Tamil kings were considered godlike. The right to the throne followed the female line, and marriages were made among cousins. (The Tamils were alarmed by arranged marriages in northern India in which young girls were sent to live with strangers.)

Generous sea access made the Tamils wealthy merchants. It also provided peaceful contact with Rome, Egypt, Bali, Sumatra, and Java. The Tamils traded spices, teak, ivory, exotic birds, onyx, jewels, cotton, and silk for gold. Along with Tamil goods, Indian religion, philosophy, and Ayurvedic medicine (the ancient Hindu science of health) were transported beyond the Indian world.

St. Thomas the Apostle brought Christianity to southern India in AD 52. He landed at Kerala and, according to local history, was martyred in AD 68. A small community of Christians remains in the area today. An even smaller community of Jews in Cochin may also date to the first century.

The three southern kingdoms unified against northern attacks. Otherwise, they fought among themselves. In the fourth century, the Pallava, or "robber," dynasty usurped the Cholas. Their reign produced some of southern India's most splendid architecture. They built numerous *gopurams*, or gateways, to temples that still stand today.

Medieval India and the Mughal Empire

India's medieval period spanned the seventh to thirteenth centuries. While southern India remained peaceful, the Rajput kings controlled northern India and were almost constantly at war with one another. These conflicts distracted the Rajput warriors—an army that included women—from the approach of the Muslim Turks, who, like the Mongols, invaded the region from time to time.

This towering *gopuram*, or gateway, is located at the Sri Meenakshi Sundareswarar Temple in Madurai, the oldest city in Tamil Nadu. The Pandya dynasty of South India grew wealthy from the trade of silk, pearls, and spices, which financed the building of fantastic temples. Sri Meenakshi is a major pilgrimage site, and roughly 15,000 people a day converge there to view its brightly colored, mythological sculptures and to participate in temple festivals.

TIMUR~BEK *ou le grand* TAMERLAN,
Empereur du mogol.
Tire de l'Histoire du Voyage
A Paris chez Duflos rue St Victor. A.P.D.R.

This engraving shows an elegantly dressed Timur, emperor of the Mongols, and was printed by Pierre Duflos in 1780. Timur invaded Delhi in 1398, reducing the city to ruins and exporting its treasures back to his home in Samarkand. Timur later sacked Baghdad and Damascus, creating an expansive territory that was controlled under the Mughal Empire for centuries.

Between 1000 and 1026, a Turk named Mahmud of Ghazni repeatedly attacked Punjab. His most famous battle destroyed and looted the Somnath Temple. In 1191, Rajput Prithviraja III defeated another Turk, Muhammad Ghuri, in the Battle of Tarain, but he died the following year. The Turks took power and founded the Delhi Sultanate.

The first dynasty of the Delhi Sultanate was called the Slave Dynasty. Most of its officials were Turkish *mamluks*, or warrior slaves. These men became military leaders, governors, and court officers. One of the sultanate's rulers, Raziya, was the first woman ruler in the Islamic world.

By 1290, Indian Muslims had replaced the slaves of the sultanate. For most of the thirteenth century, the sultanate struggled with eastern and southern Hindu kingdoms. Then, Alauddin Khalji took power. In 1299, he conquered Gujarat. By 1311, he had conquered four of the major Hindu fortresses in Rajasthan. His southern raids won him territory beyond the Narmada River. He demanded tribute (taxes) from as far south as the Pandya kingdom.

The sultanate expanded until the reign of Muhammad bin Tughlaq (1324–1351). Bin Tughlaq tried to rule Hindu India and also attack the Mongols to the north. To pay for this, he taxed the Indian peasants, who revolted. Unable to maintain control over its subjects, the sultanate began to disintegrate. In 1398, the Asian conqueror Timur (also known as Timur the Lame, or Tamerlane) sacked Delhi

In 1590, the Mughal emperor Akbar commissioned a book called the *Akbarnama*, which documented his reign. This miniature painting from the *Akbarnama* shows Akbar as a fierce hunter, an image that shows his bravery as he rides the wild elephant over a collapsing bridge. The *Akbarnama* is now located in the Victoria and Albert Museum in London, England.

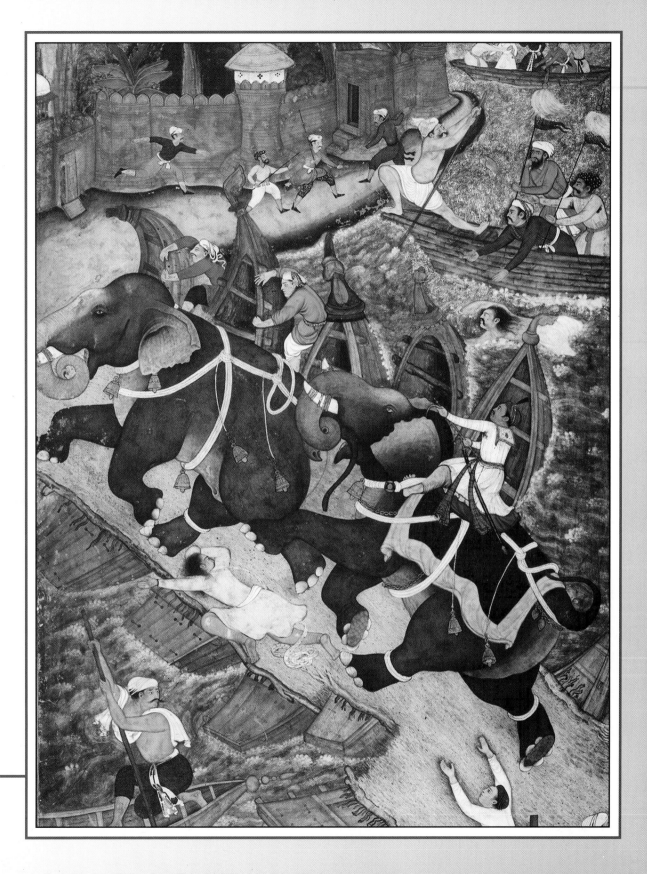

and finished off the sultanate. New kingdoms flourished across the region with Hindus dominating the south and Muslims competing for power in the north.

In 1526, Timur's descendant, Babur, took control of Delhi and Agra and founded the Mughal Empire (1526–1707). Babur's grandson, Akbar, unified most of central and northern India. During the 1580s and 1590s, Akbar expanded India's northwestern territories through Afghanistan, using its major cities as frontier fortresses. In the east, he occupied territories through much of Bengal. To the south, he held Gujarat and central India. Mughals ruled all of India north of the Godavari River. When Akbar died in 1605, he left a politically stable empire. The highly cultured Mughal court encouraged poetry, painting, and architecture.

Akbar's success was partly due to sensible taxation policies. Local landowners, or *zamindars*, made money from the peasants who worked their land, but they paid only part of it to the state. More important, Akbar was careful not to alienate Hindus. He promoted religious tolerance and ended the *jizya* tax on non-Muslims. He also prevented his men from forcibly converting prisoners of war to Islam. Akbar's policies on land ownership were so effective that the *zamindari* system continued through the middle of the twentieth century.

In the late fifteenth century, beginning with the explorer Vasco da Gama in 1498, the Portuguese arrived in India. They traded for spices, which they sold at home for mammoth profits. In Europe, black pepper was known as "black gold." In 1510, the Portuguese built a base at Goa, midway along India's western coast. Until 1961, Goa remained under Portuguese rule.

The Portuguese monopoly lasted a century. Then other European traders arrived. The Dutch East India Company traded throughout the East Indies for tea, silk, and spices. Their success intrigued the British. Stories of floating marble palaces, gardens of brightly colored peacocks, and jewels the size of ostrich eggs trickled back to England. By 1600, Queen Elizabeth I gave the

Vasco de Gama led the expedition that took the Portuguese to India in 1498. Through naval superiority, the Portuguese established a shipping empire in the Indian Ocean. They erected military forts around India's coastlines to protect their enterprise and exported Indian spices back to Portugal, which made them wealthy. The Portuguese also sent Christian missionaries to India in an attempt to gain converts to the Roman Catholic faith.

British East India Company the right to trade in India. Eight years later, the company landed in Gujarat.

In 1658, Aurangzeb became the Mughal emperor. For ten years, he expanded the empire steadily. Then he began to enforce Islamic law, or *sharia*. He replaced Hindus in government positions with Muslims. His tax collectors brought back the jizya tax. All this antagonized his Hindu allies and fractured the kingdom. When Aurangzeb died in 1707, the Mughal Empire was still powerful, but it declined in only a few decades under his weak successors.

The British East India Company

During Aurangzeb's rule, the British created trading capitals at Madras (Chennai) in 1640, at Bombay (Mumbai) in 1668, and at Calcutta in 1690. They sent cotton, silk, saltpeter, and indigo home to Europe. Opium from Indian-grown poppies allowed them to trade with China for tea—already a British necessity. The British paid for goods in silver and copper. This money was essential to the struggling Mughals.

In 1765, the now-powerless Mughal emperor gave the British East India Company control of the land around Calcutta. Outside of Bengal, British power was unofficial. Usually, the company offered local princes military protection for money. This money supported the British military, increasing the size of its army. The Indian rulers grew poorer. Some rebelled. Others collapsed.

In the south, Tipu Sultan, known as the Tiger of Mysore, and his father, Haider Ali, fought for Mysore's freedom.

The success of Dutch and Portuguese traders in tea, spice, and other luxury goods inspired Queen Elizabeth I of England to establish the British East India Trading Company on mainland India. Pictured here is an illustration taken from the 1727 book *Voyages* by Jean Albert de Mandelslo, depicting the British trading station of Surat. The British built fortified settlements to isolate themselves from the Indian population and to protect their goods.

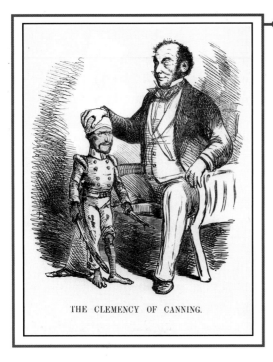

THE CLEMENCY OF CANNING.

This political cartoon portrays Earl Charles Canning, the governor general of India, belittling a sepoy soldier during the time of the Sepoy Revolt in 1857. The cartoon documents the tension in Anglo-Indian relations. When sepoys learned that the ends of their new Enfield rifle cartridges were lined with animal fat, they staged a revolt. The unclean ammunition was later recalled.

They modernized their army and won several victories. In 1799, the British defeated them. That same year, the Sikh leader Ranjit Singh captured Lahore and created a Sikh state in Punjab. The British made a truce with Singh in 1802. They focused on subduing the northwestern Marathas. In the wars of 1816–1818, they quelled the Maratha armies. Afterward, they returned to Punjab and fought two wars with the Sikhs. By 1849, Punjab was in British hands.

The Mughals had ruled most, but not all, of India. Hyderabad and Kashmir were both large, independent kingdoms. Numerous Rajput *maharajas* (Hindu princes) and Muslim *nawabs* (wealthy landowners), as well as a few last Maratha chieftains, ruled their own princely states. Altogether, there were 600 independent rulers. Rather than wage war on all of them, the British simply taxed them.

Outside the kings' territories, everything was British-controlled. Within their states, they were independent.

For the most part, the British did not interfere with Indian religions.

This engraving, now housed in Delhi, illustrates the capture of Bahadur Shah II in 1857. Captain William Hodson was the commander of the British cavalry that reoccupied Delhi and forced Bahadur's surrender at Humayoun's Tomb. This event crushed the "Indian Mutiny" and was effectively the end of the Mughal Empire.

This title page for the 1859 book *Campaign in India 1857–58* by George F. Atkinson recalls the era of the "Indian Mutiny." It shows sepoys at rifle practice during the time of the rebellion. While the British considered the rebellion an act of disloyalty, many Indians viewed it as the first step toward a national liberation movement for India. Indians refer to the conflict as the First War of Independence.

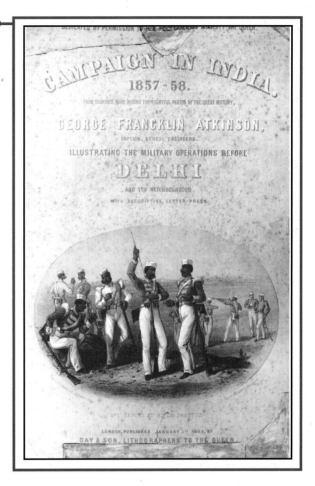

Governor-General William Bentinck did outlaw human sacrifice. The British also tried to stop *sati*, in which a widow threw herself, alive, into the fire of her dead husband's funeral pyre to show her devotion to him. Beyond this, the British believed they left the customs and culture of India intact. However, unlike Akbar (who translated Hindu texts into Persian to promote Hindu-Muslim understanding), British tolerance was a form of indifference and insensitivity.

The Sepoy Revolt of 1857 took the British completely by surprise. Known as the First War of Independence in India, the British called it the "Indian Mutiny." Indians who worked as foot soldiers for the British army were called sepoys. At that time, a new British rifle used cartridges (the ends of which soldiers bit off before loading) greased with pork and beef fat. For Muslims, pork fat was unclean. For Hindus, the use of beef fat desecrated the sacred cow. In Meerut, near Delhi, the news took hold in a day. Forty-seven battalions turned on the British army. They declared their support for the last Mughal emperor, the eighty-year-old Bahadur Shah II.

It took six months and the help of the northern Sikhs for the British to regain control. In January 1858, they reclaimed Delhi and banished Bahadur Shah. Queen Victoria dismissed the British East India Company, declared herself sovereign empress of India, and appointed a viceroy to govern the country.

"There is no article like salt, outside water, by taxing which the state can reach even the starving millions, the sick, the maimed, and the utterly helpless. The tax institutes therefore the most inhuman poll tax the ingenuity of man can devise," said Indian nationalist Mohandas Gandhi in response to the British salt tax. Gandhi, pictured here with poet and politician Sarojini Naidu, led the month-long salt march from Ahmedabad to the Gujarat coast, which initiated India's civil disobedience movement.

Independence

For the next ninety years, India lived under the British raj, or rule. Britain treated the country as a bottomless well of raw materials. It increased iron and coal mining; farmed tea, coffee, and cotton plantations; built roads and railways; and erected telegraph poles. The British also built schools to educate some Indians to work in their government offices.

Indians in these schools noticed that English "democracy" existed in Britain but not in British India. Other Indians pointed out that India was home to cities 2,000 years older than Rome. The Indian middle classes began to question foreign rule.

In 1885, the Indian National Congress (INC), which was to be at the forefront of the national movement for independence, was founded. The INC wanted self-rule. In 1906, the All-India Muslim League formed. They felt that the INC was a Hindu group and would not represent Muslims fairly.

In 1915, an Indian lawyer named Mohandas Karamchand Gandhi advised the INC to

Here we see a salt raid on the Wadela salt pans in 1930 by members of the Indian National Congress. Loyalists to the British raj, however, were not as taken with Gandhi's principles of non-violence and are shown in this photograph swinging a baton into the crowd.

This resolution passed by Pandit Motilal Nehru is from the organizational plan of the independence movement. In 1928, the All-Parties Conference appointed Nehru, a lawyer, to head a committee that would draft a constitution for post-colonial India. It outlines the details of a parliamentary style government, with rules for representing the various territories in a unified India.

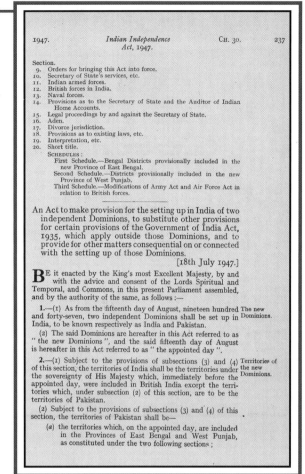

broaden its membership. The INC should be an all-India party. Every Indian, whether poor, rural, illiterate, or of "unclean" caste had the right to join the INC. Gandhi also urged women to participate in politics.

Gandhi did not wish to wage a military war with the British. He believed in the idea of *ahimsa*, or nonviolence. He began a series of passive resistance, or *satyagraha*, protests. One of the most effective was *hartal*, or strike. In hartal, participators refused to work. When this happened, the government could not function. He also fasted to persuade Hindus and Muslims to join together against the British. People called him Mahatma, which means "great soul."

It was clear to Gandhi that the British were in India for money. He campaigned against products that made money for the British. The British taxed Indian salt. Gandhi urged people not to buy it. He led a march to the sea so that people could gather free salt from the ocean. Gandhi also refused to wear British cloth. He learned to spin cotton into thread and wore only hand-woven cloth, or *khadi*.

As part of the passive resistance movement, immense groups of people gathered peacefully, but illegally, to protest wrongs. When armed troops ordered them to leave, men, women, and children sat calmly and refused to do so. In 1919, General Reginald Dyer ordered his troops to open fire on a peaceful protest meeting in Amritsar. His men killed 379 people and wounded 1,200. This hideous decision lost the British even

RECD. NO. B. 1065

INSURANCE
Nothing can take the place of one's own country. ONE'S OWN INSURANCE COMPANIES are the BEST.

The Bombay Chronicle

FOUNDED BY SIR PHIROZESHAH M. MEHTA IN 1913

INSURANCE
SWADESHI in INSURANCe is easy. INDIAN INSURANCE COMPANIES are ready with their service.

VOL. XX NO. 219   BOMBAY TUESDAY, SEPTEMBER 13, 1932   PRICE ONE ANNA.

GANDHI'S FIRM RESOLVE TO "FAST UNTO DEATH"

Self-Immolation On Behalf Of "Depressed" Classes

STEP FORCED UPON HIM BY PREMIER'S AWARD

Senses Poison In Exclusion Of Depressed Classes From General Electorate

SCATHING INDICTMENT OF "GO VERNMENT TERRORISM"

SIMLA, Sept. 12.

MAHATMA GANDHI'S DECISION TO FAST HIMSELF TO DEATH IS CONVEYED IN CORRESPONDENCE JUST RELEASED BETWEEN HIM AND SIR SAMUEL HOARE AND THE PREMIER.

He wrote a letter to Sir Samuel Hoare on the 11th March stating that he would starve himself to death if the grant of separate electorates to the Hindu Community was dissected by the "Depressed" classes to the Government and he has now intimated to the Government that while many other parts of the Communal Decision, they do not warrant such self-immolation as he proposed by going on fast on the 20th September and which fast he would continue even if he is released.

WAY TO STOP THE FAST.

The only way to stop the fast would be for the Government to revise the decision by including the "Depressed" classes in the General Electorate under a common franchise, no matter how wide it is.

The Premier's reply regrets that Government's decision cannot be changed except under conditions laid down in that decision.

GANDHIJI–HOARE–PREMIER CORRESPONDENCE RELEASED

SIMLA Sept. 12.

Letter from Mahatma Gandhi to Sir Samuel Hoare, dated Yeravda Central Prison, March 11th 1932.

Dear Sir Samuel,

I AM ONE OF THEM

Mahatma Gandhi

SIMLA SHOCKED AT GANDHI BOMBSHELL

Rajah Tables Adjournment Of Assembly

(From Our Special Correspondent)

SIMLA, Sept. 12.

The correspondence between Mahatma Gandhi, Sir Samuel Hoare and Mr. Ramsay MacDonald in which Mahatmaji intimates his decision to fast himself unto death from 20th September in case the Communal Award is not revised in respect of the "Depressed Classes" was circulated to the members of the Assembly at this evening.

EMERGENCY MEETING OF VICEROY'S CABINET CALLED

(From Our Special Correspondent)

SIMLA, Sept. 12.

STOP PRESS

"GOVERNMENT LIKELY TO RELEASE HIM."

SIMLA, Sept. 12.

MR. RAMSAY MACDONALD

LIVING UP TO HIS WORDS

Gandhi's London Speech Recalled

REICHSTAG DISSOLVED

HINDENBURG'S DECISION

LONDON, Sept. 12.

Berlin.—President Hindenburg has dissolved the Reichstag.—Reuter.

Von Papen Presents Ominous Red Portfolio

LONDON Sept 12

SOCIALIST MOVE

LONDON, Sept 12

Force if Necessary To Dissolve Reichstag

LONDON, Sept. 12.

NO SOFT BARGAIN WITH BRITAIN

De Valera Confident Of Winning Fight For Land Annuities

LONDON, Sept 12

PARLIAMENT TO REASSEMBLE ON OCT. 27

LONDON, Sept. 12.

CONGRESS BULLETIN "PRESS" TRACED TO MULUND

Sequel To Arrest Of Young Men Near Wilson College

This political cartoon reflects the need for strategic movements to undermine British authority in India. It involves pitting segments of the population against one another. Here we see Gandhi making the first move, much to the surprise of Britain.

INDIA—A CHESSBOARD

more support, swelling the ranks of the INC.

Led by Jawaharlal Nehru, the INC represented much of India but was still at loggerheads with the Muslim League. Gandhi had called for the British to "Quit India." The Muslim League's Mohammed Ali Jinnah answered with the slogan "Divide and Quit."

Jinnah wanted a separate Muslim state. This was called Partition. Gandhi did not like the idea. Nehru accepted it reluctantly. Jinnah believed it was the only way. He drew borders to create West Pakistan (now Pakistan) and East Pakistan (now Bangladesh) on either side of Punjab. At midnight on August 14, 1947, the British returned India to the Indians and Partition came into effect.

The Republic of India

There were thirty-five million Muslims in India and several million Hindus in Pakistan. After Partition, more than ten million people moved in each direction across Punjab. It was the largest human migration in history. The resulting violence was gruesome. Hindus attacked Muslims. Muslims ambushed convoys of Hindu trucks. Whole villages burned to the ground. Between two hundred thousand and one million people died.

Gandhi went on a hunger strike to protest the violence. On January 30, 1948, he was assassinated by a Hindu extremist. This vicious act shocked the nation into a cease-fire. Indians of every religion had had deep respect for the Mahatma. Jawaharlal Nehru, now India's first prime minister, told the country, "The light has gone out of our lives."

This September 1932 edition of the *Bombay Chronicle* reported on Gandhi's hunger strike and indicated the growing visibility of his tactics for peaceful social change in India. Gandhi went on a hunger strike to protest the treatment of the Harijan, or Untouchable, caste, demanding that they gain representation in governmental matters. This action solidified support for the independence movement across class lines.

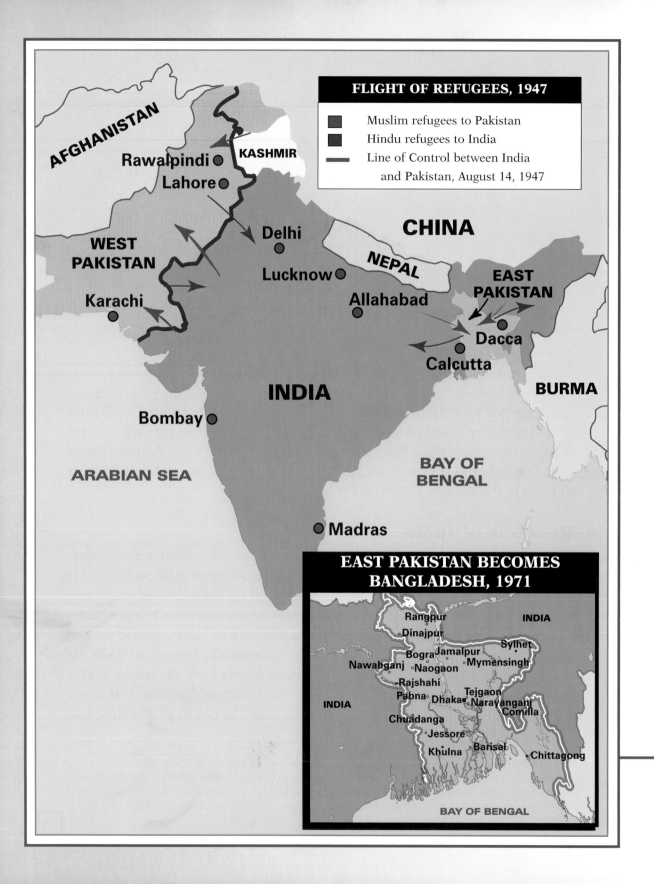

FLIGHT OF REFUGEES, 1947

Muslim refugees to Pakistan
Hindu refugees to India
Line of Control between India
and Pakistan, August 14, 1947

AFGHANISTAN

Rawalpindi
Lahore

KASHMIR

WEST
PAKISTAN

Karachi

Delhi

Lucknow

CHINA

NEPAL

Allahabad

EAST
PAKISTAN

Dacca

Calcutta

INDIA

BURMA

Bombay

ARABIAN SEA

BAY OF
BENGAL

Madras

**EAST PAKISTAN BECOMES
BANGLADESH, 1971**

Rangpur
Dinajpur

INDIA

Sylhet

Bogra Jamalpur

Nawabganj Naogaon Mymensingh

Rajshahi

Pabna Dhaka Tejgaon
Narayanganj

INDIA

Chuadanga

Comilla

Jessore

Khulna Barisal

Chittagong

BAY OF BENGAL

Shri Atal Bihari Vajpayee has been the prime minister of India since 1996. He was one of the founding fathers of the Bharatiya Janata Party (BJP), which espouses a Hindu nationalist philosophy of government.

Nehru wanted the new India to be modern, democratic, and self-sufficient. He created a series of five-year plans to encourage industry and agriculture. Two years after his death in 1964, his daughter, Indira Gandhi, was voted into office by a landslide.

Religious bitterness continued. In 1971, a civil war in East Pakistan drove nine million refugees into India. It ended with the creation of the new nation of Bangladesh. In the early 1980s, extremist Sikhs wanted to turn northern Punjab into a Sikh nation called Khalistan. They stockpiled weapons at the Golden Temple in Amritsar. Indira Gandhi ordered an attack on the temple that killed 600 people, most of them Sikhs. On October 31, 1984, two of her Sikh security guards assassinated her.

Today, India's prime minister is Atal Bihari Vajpayee. A member of the national movement while in college, he studied political science and law and then became a journalist. Active in parliament for four decades, he was first elected prime minister in 1996. A deep believer in social equality and women's rights, Vajpayee sees India as a progressive nation built on thousands of years of civilization.

Tensions between Hindus and Muslims were further exacerbated during Partition, when millions migrated between newly independent India and the divided sections of East and West Pakistan. By 1971, Bengalis in East Pakistan forced secession to create an independent nation of Bangladesh, show in the inset map *(bottom)*.

THE INDIAN LANGUAGES

3

From Ancient Sanskrit to Modern Hindi

I ndians speak many languages. Before independence in 1947, Indians spoke as many as fifteen major languages and 1,652 minor languages and dialects. After independence, India organized itself regionally, according to its languages and culture. Modern Indian districts share a government but have their own cultural traditions, including independent languages. India's two official languages are Hindi and English.

Indo-Aryan

Nearly half of the people in modern India (roughly 500 million) speak either Hindi or Bengali. Telugu, Punjabi, Tamil, Marathi, and Urdu are also widely spoken, each by approximately fifty million people.

India's primary languages, like Hindi, Bengali, and Urdu, are Indo-Aryan languages and share grammatical features with European languages. These languages date to the Aryan conquerors of 1500 BC. In the 3,500 years that followed the Aryan invasion, their language absorbed words and structures from Indian languages. This created the Indo-Aryan group of languages.

In this street scene in Old Delhi *(left)*, we see both Hindi and English written on billboards. The migration of many different ethnic groups throughout the country has left a mark in the variety of languages spoken in India. Reading the scriptures is an important part of the *sadhu's*, or holy man's, routine. This sadhu in Calcutta *(above)* spends his day contemplating books from the Vedas. The Vedas were originally composed in Sanskrit, one of the earliest Indo-Aryan languages. Sanskrit evolved so that Brahmin priests from different places could communicate in a common language.

On the left a Hindu reads a newspaper written in Hindi, and on the right a Muslim reads a paper written in Urdu. Both languages are commonly spoken and understood in India, but they are written in different scripts. Urdu uses a script that bears a strong resemblance to that of Arabic, while Hindi characters are written in a style known as Devanagari.

The Aryans' sacred texts, the Vedas, were written in old Indo-Aryan. The classical form of this language is Sanskrit. This was the official language of learning, writing, and government. In the fifth century BC, scholars developed formal grammatical rules for Sanskrit. Until AD 1000, it was India's most important scholarly language. Sanskrit ceased to be the language of court and state when the Persian-speaking Muslims invaded India. Today, Sanskrit, like Latin, is a language used for study rather than for speaking. Sometimes these are referred to as "dead" languages.

Hindi and Urdu

While the British ruled India, they tried to establish a nationalized school system. The number of different languages made it difficult to print textbooks. The British attempted to standardize unusual dialects into a single language. They gathered a wide range of dialects and "corrected" their various spellings,

The elephant-headed deity Ganesh is pictured here in this primary source derived from an illustrated children's book. Ganesh has ties to language and writing, as it is retold in the legend that Ganesh broke off his own tusk and used it to write down the epic Mahabharata.

grammar, and vocabulary to make them agree.

British rule began in the northeastern region of Bengal. Over time it moved west to Punjab, home to Delhi. People in Delhi spoke Khari Boli, a language the British called Hindustani. It used an Indo-Aryan grammatical structure and numerous Persian "loan-words." The Muslims liked Hindustani because these borrowed words linked it to Persian. They wrote the language in a Persian script and called it Urdu. They wanted Urdu to be the primary language of Indian Muslims.

The Indian Hindus in the north disliked this idea. They used a language they called Hindi. This was a version of Hindustani influenced by Sanskrit, the same way that Urdu was influenced by Persian. Hindi speakers used the Devanagari script, not the Persian. They claimed Hindi was the product of centuries of Hindu culture.

Since Partition, when India split into secular (mostly Hindu) India and Muslim Pakistan, Hindi has been India's national language, while Urdu is the official language of Pakistan. For common purposes, these languages are similar. People can easily

An exit sign written in English and Hindi indicates the prominence of both languages in India, but each region has its own dialect. In the south, Dravidian languages such as Tamil are more common than Hindi. Using English is sometimes an easier way to communicate with Indians who have different native tongues.

Pictured here is a Buddhist scroll. Some of the oldest Buddhist texts in the world were produced in India, such as the Gandharan Buddhist texts from the fifth century AD. Written on birch bark in the ancient Kharosthi script, they were discovered inside a set of clay pots in the Bamiyan cave complex of Afghanistan.

chat with neighbors across the India-Pakistan border. However, different scripts mean they cannot read each other's letters.

Despite Hindi's official status, Indians still speak hundreds of dialects. Bengali, spoken by nearly 200 million people, is the most important and developed of these dialects. It is the official language of Bangladesh.

In western India, differences between Muslims and Hindus keep the languages more separate. The Punjabi dialect exists in both countries, but in Pakistan, it is more like Urdu, and in India, it is more like Hindi.

Southern Tongues

Northern India has endured invasion and conflict for more than 3,000 years. The south, which is insulated by northern India and by the ocean, has always been more stable. Southern India's Dravidian languages predate the Aryan invasion. A major language group in their own right, Dravidian languages are still spoken today.

Dravidian languages have a distinctive sound system and grammatical structure. The oldest documents show that Sanskrit is the only foreign language that has had a real impact on the Dravidian languages. Otherwise, the Dravidian dialects are still very pure. Geographically, this makes sense. Speakers of Dravidian languages did not experience the Muslim invasions. For them, Persian never had the cultural importance that it did for northern Indians.

Tamil is the southernmost and purest Dravidian language. It is spoken in Tamil Nadu, which shares the tip of the Indian peninsula with the smaller area of Kerala. Tamil is also spoken in northern Sri Lanka. The language spoken in Kerala, in the southwest, is Malayalam, which was a dialect of Tamil until the fourteenth century. Kannada and Telugu date back to AD 1000. They are spoken, respectively, to the northwest and northeast of Tamil Nadu. Like Malayalam, they are less pure examples of Dravidian languages than Tamil.

Ancient Scripts

India uses various scripts to write its many languages. In fact, no other country in the modern world has as many alphabets. Each is important to the people who use it. As with spoken language, it is difficult to force people to give up a part of their culture. Standardizing a script sometimes means homogenizing the details of many different languages into one alphabet.

India's earliest writing may be traced to the pictographs on the square white seals of the Harappans. Pictographs are

This stone seal is imprinted with a unicorn and Harappan pictographs. It is a source of the written language of Mohenjo-Daro and is now located in the National Museum of Pakistan in Karachi. Hundreds of such seals were unearthed throughout the Indus Valley.

The writing pictured here comes from a pillar in Sarnath, Varansi, and illustrates the Brahmi script. The emperor Asoka introduced Buddhism to India during his reign from 273 to 232 BC. He popularized the religion by issuing edicts concerning moral behavior, which were then carved onto stone pillars.

pictures or symbols that represent objects or ideas. Languages usually progress from simple pictures, like cave paintings, to pictographs, which can be linked to create thoughts. No one has deciphered the Harappans' pictographs. Because there are very few repetitions, the seals may be a listing of people's names, rather than common words or gods.

After the Harappans, there is a gap until the emergence of the Brahmi script of the third century BC. This comes from the reign of the Buddhist emperor Asoka. To communicate with his subjects, Asoka carved edicts (laws) onto stone pillars. These carvings represent an early form of mass communication that Asoka had used throughout his immense kingdom, from Afghanistan in the north to Mysore in the south.

The script on Asoka's pillars was sophisticated. It read from left to right and was alphabetic, not pictographic. Alphabetic letters are phonetic; they represent sounds. There is no literal connection between letters and objects. For example, instead of using a drawing of a chair to mean the word "chair," an alphabet uses letters that make up the sounds a person makes when saying "chair."

During the reign of Asoka, Indian grammar reached the point where it could communicate detailed Indo-Aryan sounds. It linked one sound to one symbol. This allowed readers to sound out words from phonetic symbols. It also meant that a handful of symbols could make every word. A pictographic system needs thousands of symbols because every object in the universe needs its own. Asoka's Brahmi script had one symbol for each consonant and one for each vowel. The Brahmi alphabet was so successful that the southern Dravidians adapted the idea to their own languages.

Modern Scripts

Over the centuries, hundreds of Indian scripts emerged. Standardized schoolbooks and government rulings have lowered this number to eleven. Modern Hindi uses Devanagari, which means "the script of the city of the gods." Devanagari has existed for more than a thousand years and is used to write Hindi, Marathi, Nepali, and Sanskrit, which makes it India's religious script. In Gujarat, just south of Pakistan, people write in a script that has long served merchants, the Gurmukhi script of the Sikhs.

Urdu is the only Indian language that uses a non-Brahmi script. When Muslims first entered India, they used a Persian script. Unlike Indian scripts, Arabic and Persian scripts are written and read right to left. Later, India's Muslim rulers continued to use this Persian script because of its link with Islam. Islamic cultural history is so important to the Muslims that Persian remains the official script in Pakistan.

English Words in Hindi

yes: haan
no: naheen
okay: achha
very good: bahut accha
bad: kharab
big: bada
small: chhota
beautiful: sundar
please: kripaya
thank you: dhanyavad, shukriya
excuse me: maaf karna
tea: chai
sari: saree
money: paysaa
school: skool
book: kitaab
water: paani
food: khaana

وچون بالها فراز کرد و خواست که رامچند و طمرو انیز در قید خود پیارد و بدیشان گفت شماه کیستد

[د]چگل من قدم می هند رامچند بعد ازپیان حسب نسب نام و نشان خودگفت سیتا را او بردا زنده

برده است و مالطلب او می رویم و بماجد داری که ما را بنجانی و در میان ما و توهیچ عداوتی نیست

او گفت چو درمقصد عداوت ندانستید سلاح را برای جبد ردست آورده اید که آنجا حاکمان بدینشا

می شود و رامچند گفت زهی جاه ته که ما را برای جاد ننمی افزاید ما را و زهی بهیش آمده است و آن ما را

خاری در دل ما می ناید او بری ایشان هرجند سخنان نزگفت سده فایده نداد و آن کسید می گفت که مرا

INDIAN MYTHS AND LEGENDS

4

o impart a society's traditions, values, history, and religious beliefs, mythological stories and legends are told and retold throughout the history of that society. Beginning with the hymns of the Rig Veda around 1200 BC, mythology has earned a permanent place in Indian culture.

India has two great epic legends, the Mahabharata and the Ramayana. In each, kings, queens, wise men, soldiers, and villains face challenges and make decisions. Their brave or cowardly acts illustrate Hindu ideas of intelligence, passion, loyalty, and immorality. The epics also explore the meaning of human existence. In conversations with mortals, gods answer questions about life, death, and duty, or *dharma*.

The Mahabharata

The Mahabharata ("Great Epic of the Bharata Dynasty"), the story of a prolonged war, began as 3,000 Sanskrit stanzas. Over several hundred years, Brahmin priests and writers added pages of religious discussion. By AD 400, it was 100,000 stanzas long. Today it remains the longest poem in the world.

During this period, Brahminism evolved into Hinduism. The much-loved Hindu god Krishna first appears in the Mahabharata. He advises the human Pandavas in their righteous war against their demon cousins, the Kauravas. By helping the Pandavas defeat their cousins, Krishna shows himself to be an incarnation of Vishnu, the Hindu god who keeps order in the world.

This folio *(left)*, an illustration taken from a sixteenth-century Persian edition of the Ramayana, is part of a collection of the Smithsonian Institution in Washington, D.C. Here *(above)* we see an illustration from the epic poem Mahabharata. The Hindu god Krishna counsels Arjuna during archery practice. Arjuna is a legendary warrior and master archer from the Pandava clan, but he has doubts about taking arms against his cousins, the Kauravas, in a civil war. Krishna reads him sacred text from the Bhagavad Gita to convince Arjuna it is his duty, or *dharma*, to participate in this battle.

At the heart of the Mahabharata lie themes of jealousy and deception. In this illustration by Nandalal Bose from *Myths of Hindus and Buddhists*, we see the Pandavan princes in the House of Lac. Their uncle Duryodhana of the Kaurava clan built them a palace made of combustible material, or Lac, as Duryodhana planned to set fire to the palace while they slept. He hoped to ensure that none of the princes would come to power as king.

The Mahabharata describes the bitter rivalry between King Kuru's two sons. The elder, Dhritarashtra, is blind and has one hundred sons, the Kauravas. Pandu, the younger, has five sons, the Pandavas. After losing a contest to the Pandavas, the Kauravas burn down the house where the Pandavas are sleeping. The Pandavas escape and hide in a nearby forest.

Eventually, the Pandavas and Kauravas reconcile and split Kuru's kingdom. Soon, however, the oldest Pandava, Yudhishthira, names himself ruler of the world. This enrages the Kauravas. Determined to win the kingdom back, they challenge Yudhishthira to a game of dice. The Kauravas are very good gamblers and Yudhishthira soon loses the kingdom. Then he gambles and loses his brothers. Finally, he gambles and loses his wife. Forced into exile with his brothers, Yudhishthira plots his revenge.

Twelve years later, the Pandavas return from exile and attack the Kauravas. They fight for eighteen days. The sight of his uncles and cousins killing each other drives the Pandava hero, Arjuna, to despair. Krishna reminds Arjuna that battle is a warrior's duty, or dharma. Speaking as Vishnu, he describes the war as part of the cycle of life and rebirth that will eventually lead Arjuna to heaven. This portion of the Mahabharata is called the Bhagavad Gita and teaches Hindu ideas of fate, duty, and union with god. The five Pandavas win the war, but when they claim their victory, they discover that all one hundred Kauravas and all of their own sons are dead.

The Ramayana

The Ramayana is less grand in scope, though more spiritual, than the Mahabharata. It praises the loyalty and sense of duty that creates strong human

This seventeenth-century Deccan-style illustration is a primary source from the Ramayana, one of India's most sacred epic poems. Here we see Hanuman, the monkey general, discovering Sita, the wife of Rama. She is being held in Sri Lanka by the demon Ravana, who has fallen in love with her.

bonds. Only 25,000 stanzas, it is probably the work of a single writer, a wise man named Valmiki. It is more elegantly written than the many-authored Mahabharata.

Ramayana means "Rama's Way" or the "Romance of Rama." The epic tells the story of Prince Rama's exile from Ayodhya. Rama is the son of King Dasharatha. As the story opens, the king decides to pass his crown to his beloved son Rama to the delight of Rama's mother and the king's other two wives.

After the announcement, an old nursemaid convinces the king's youngest wife that her son should instead be king. This queen saved the king's life during a battle against the demons of drought. He repaid her with two favors. The queen uses these favors to drive Rama from Ayodhya and take the throne for her own son.

The exiled Rama enters the forest with his wife, Sita, and his brother, the warrior Laksmana. Soon, Rama, Laksmana, and Sita build a small house in the forest and live there quietly.

Sita remains in the house with Laksmana for protection, but the demon king Ravana sees her and falls in love. Determined to win her adoration, Ravana tricks Laksmana into leaving Sita alone. He then abducts Sita and takes her to his kingdom in Lanka (Sri Lanka).

When Rama learns of Sita's kidnapping, he is devastated. With the help of Laksmana, he rallies a large army of monkeys, the most important being Rama's faithful devotee, Hanuman. With the help of Hanuman and the monkey army, Rama attacks Ravana's walled city in Lanka (Sri Lanka), kills Ravana, and rescues Sita. After their victory, Rama, Sita, and Laksmana ride home in triumph. With his new army behind him, Rama reclaims Ayodhya from his brother and becomes king.

The Lion and the Jackals

Once upon a time, a lion king known as Singh Rajah ruled an immense land where his animal subjects lived in fear. The sound of his roar turned their bones to jelly. At dusk, when he roused himself to hunt, panthers trembled. When he yawned and shook his mane, monkeys shrieked. Weasels and badgers shrank in their holes and deer fled before him. But Singh Rajah was so fast that he pounced and devoured them.

After a time, there were only two animals left in the entire kingdom. These were Raja Jackal and Rani Jackal, the jackal king and queen. They were faster and smarter than the other animals. Every day they ran as far from the sleeping lion as they could. Soon, they were exhausted. At last, they sat down at the base of a tree to think of a plan for survival.

At nightfall, the lion's roar rolled across the jungle. Exhausted from running Raja Jackal decided to travel instead to the lion king's side, along with his wife.

Soon they arrived at the lion's den. Singh Rajah was terrible to behold. His mane stood wild and his teeth shone in the darkness. When he saw the two jackals, he grinned and roared horribly before he leapt toward them. "I will be so happy to eat you!" he said.

Just then Raja Jackal said, "Oh, Your Highness, we have been running from a raja much more terrifying than you!" The lion stopped. "What do you mean? I am the most powerful raja in the land!" Rani Jackal said, "Well yes, Sire, it is true that you are very horrible. You have eaten everyone in the kingdom. But the fact is, this new raja is a thousand times more terrifying. I am afraid, Sire, even you will be nothing before him." The lion looked irritated. He replied, "Take me to him so that I may kill him!"

Together they trotted out of the den and down the hill to a large well. They put their forepaws on the stone lip and peered inside. Raja Jackal said, "This is where he lives." Singh Rajah pushed the two jackals away and leapt on to the well's ledge. As he peered inside, he saw a face as wild as his own. He roared to frighten his opponent. As he did so, the lion in the well roared right back.

Incensed, Singh Rajah leapt into the well, plunging into its watery depths. Enraged at the jackals' treachery, the lion howled. He struggled to leap back out of the well, but its sides were too steep. Finally, his great strength was defeated and he died.

Adapted from the Panchatantra

These revelers have formed a human pyramid in honor of the birthday of Lord Krishna, part of the festival of Govinda. The myth states that the precocious Lord Krishna loved curd so much that he stole the tasty treat, which was hung off the ground in earthen pots. His friends helped him form a human pyramid to break the pots and claim their contents.

Indian Humor

Some of India's most beloved stories are animal fables. Long before Greece's Aesop, India had the Panchatantra and the Hitopadesa. Passed orally from one storyteller to another, the eighty-seven fables of the Panchatantra were finally written down in Kashmir in the second century BC.

Scholars debate whether India's animal fables influenced Aesop. Many Western animal fables use lions, tigers, monkeys, and elephants as characters, much like the Indian tales did. All of these animals are common in India, but extremely rare in Europe.

The Panchatantra was translated into Persian in the sixth century and into Arabic in the eighth century. Its stories spread from the Islamic world into Spain, Italy, and France and from Constantinople (Istanbul) up into eastern Europe. In 1431, a German version of a Panchatantra fable became one of the earliest printed books in Europe.

The Panchatantra opens with the story of a king whose two sons are slow at their studies. The king finds a Brahmin tutor who claims that he can teach the princes all of human knowledge, or *niti*, in six months. The tutor's lessons are the fables of the Panchatantra.

Each story in the Panchatantra has a moral. Some show that it is important to be honest, while others tell that the clever can defeat the strong. The animal characters of the Panchatantra fables represent human virtues, vices, and weaknesses. Their victories and disasters teach human listeners how to behave.

INDIAN FESTIVALS AND CEREMONIES OF ANTIQUITY AND TODAY

5

The Indian year is dense with celebrations. There are thousands of holidays, rituals, and festivals when Indians dress in brilliant colors, lead processions on the backs of elephants, and attend feasts. Most of these occasions are religious, but those celebrating Indian independence are also important.

On January 26, Republic Day celebrates the moment in 1950 that India adopted its constitution. Seventeen years before independence, India had partial control of its government, but it was still a part of the British Empire. Republic Day is a national celebration but is most dramatic in New Delhi, where camels, elephants, and floats follow a military parade. Later in the year, on August 15, India's Independence Day is celebrated. In Old Delhi, the prime minister addresses the nation from the ramparts of the Red Fort built by the Mughal emperor Shah Jahan in 1565. On October 2, the country remembers Gandhi, known as the Mahatma, or "great soul," born on that day in 1869.

Hindu Festivals

Jawaharlal Nehru once called India "a madhouse of religions" with most having ritual celebrations. The Hindus, with their endless spectrum of gods and goddesses, host the greatest variety. One of the most spectacular is the Kumbh Mela. According to Hindu tradition, the Kumbh Mela dates from the demons' theft of the gods' nectar of immortality in a vessel, or *khumbh*.

These women *(left)* are Hindu devotees who have come to Allahabad to bathe in the sacred waters where the Ganges, Yamuna, and mythical Saraswati Rivers converge. Allahabad is the holiest of the four locations to which Hindus pilgrimage in celebration of the Kumbh Mela, or Festival of the Pots. This sadhu *(above)* is practicing Hindu rituals during the Kumbh Mela in Haridwar. Many sadhus are ascetics, people who practice self-denial for religious reasons. Sadhus belong to different sects, pledging their devotion to a particular Hindu god. The colorful markings on this sadhu's forehead are called *tika*, and they indicate to which deity he is devoted.

Throughout India—with the exception of two states—slaughtering cattle is prohibited. Cows, like the painted animals in this photograph, are considered sacred. The Indian philosophy behind this idea is that cows should be worshiped because they are capable of elevating much of the physical work of mankind, thereby allowing humans the opportunity to seek higher, spiritual goals.

Enraged, the gods attacked the demons. During the battle, the nectar spilled. It fell at twelve points, eight in heaven and four on Earth. Where the nectar touched Earth, it created the four most sacred cities in the world: Allahabad, Nasik, Ujjain, and Hardwar.

The Kumbh Mela occurs every three years. In a twelve-year period, it is celebrated once at each of the four sacred cities. On festival years, astrologers track the positions of the sun and moon. When the heavens align, the sacred rivers of the year's Kumbh Mela city are believed to flow with life-preserving nectar.

Millions of pilgrims arrive to bathe in this holy water and hear the wisdom of holy men, or *sadhus*. Among the tent cities hastily built along the river, naked ascetics test themselves by dancing to exhaustion or walking on hot coals. Ash-smeared gurus preach the way to a holier life.

Apart from the Kumbh Mela, most festivals are annual. In January, southern India celebrates the harvest with Pongol or Sankranti. A three-day event in Tamil Nadu and Karnataka, Pongol is named for the sweet rice villagers cook for the occasion. They

This boy is enjoying the festival of colors during the Hindu holiday of Holi. Celebrated during the full moon at the end of the lunar year, it symbolizes the dissolution of time.

drape cattle with flowers and parade them to music. The festival ends with a rodeo. Horned bulls are decorated with money and led into a ring where brave celebrants attempt to steal the money from the animals' sharp horns.

In February, Vasant Panchami celebrates the Hindu goddess of knowledge, Saraswati. People leave pens, paintbrushes, and musical instruments at the goddess's shrines. Later in the month, Hindus honor Shiva during Shivrati. A day of fasting is followed by a day of feasting on Shiva's favorite snack foods: dates, fruits, nuts, sweet potatoes, and rice.

April brings one of the most colorful and playful of the Hindu festivals: Holi. A celebration of spring, Holi is riotously joyous. Celebrants smear and squirt each other with colorful powders and paints until everyone resembles a rainbow. The excitement of Holi, coupled with the shock of being sloshed by buckets of colored water softens usual social barriers. Caste seems less important, and men and women flirt shamelessly.

The Baisakhi Festival, in April or May, celebrates the Hindu New Year on the day the Ganges River, or the goddess Ganga, descended to Earth. Hindus travel to the river to bathe. There are processions in river towns from Srinagar's Mughal gardens in the north all the way to Tamil Nadu.

In late July, Naga Panchami honors the thousand-headed serpent Naga, on whom Vishnu reclines in contemplation. Snake charmers offer women fertility blessings. All over the country, Hindus feed milk and sweets to cobras.

On the fourth day after the August new moon, Indians celebrate Ganesh Chaturtui, the birthday of Shiva and Parvati's elephant-headed son Ganesh. The

These members of a snake-worshiping cult are attending a festival in Chakdah, West Bengal. Hindus believe that attending Naga Panchami, or the Festival of Snakes, will help abate the possibility of getting bitten during this time. To Hindus, snakes rank second only to cows in terms of sacredness.

festival at Maharashtra is particularly grand. Dussehra, the most popular festival in the country, occurs in the fall and is celebrated in various ways. In the north, revelers call it Ram Lila and play music to remember the life and exploits of Rama. In Bengal and much of eastern India, the festival is called Durga Puja, and in the south it is named Navrati, nine nights dedicated to the Mother Goddess.

The end of the year brings Diwali, or the Festival of Lights, which celebrates Rama's return to Ayodhya. People fill their houses with oil lamps and watch performances, fireworks, and light shows.

Hindu Customs

In addition to major festivals, Hindus share daily rituals and rites. In the old days there were dozens. Although many still exist today, those that celebrate birth, adulthood, marriage, parenthood, and death are considered most important.

A woman lights candles during Diwali, the Hindu festival of lights, which is dedicated to Lakshmi, the goddess of good fortune. Hindus believe Lakshmi roams the earth looking for homes that will welcome her, bringing prosperity to those who are hospitable. Hindus invite Lakshmi into their homes by placing lights on their windowsills.

The naming ceremony happens twelve days after a baby's birth. In the north, the baby swings in a bassinet as a priest lights twelve lamps. Women sing and the priest speaks aloud the baby's name. In Tamil Nadu, the baby's name is traced with a coin in a heap of rice while the baby faces east. He or she is then girdled with a thread from which dangle half a dozen gold charms.

Brahmin boys learn Sanskrit by age eight for the ceremony of the thread. A boy sits with his father close to a sacred fire. A priest places a loop of thread over the boy's head. It hangs from the left shoulder across the chest to below the right hand. The priest then recites from the Rig Veda. The father repeats the priest's words to the boy, who also recites them. Afterward, there is a party with many guests.

The most important life rite is marriage. In arranged marriages, the parents' concern is to find a match for their child socially, religiously, financially, and according to heavenly signs. The ceremony begins when the bride's parents welcome the groom and formally give him their daughter, whom he receives, along with her father.

The woman on the left is using henna, or *mehndi* in Hindi, to decorate a woman's hands. Henna can be traced back to ancient Egypt and is obtained from the plant *Lawsonia inermis*, whose twigs, leaves, and flowers are ground into a fine powder, then mixed with hot water and applied like paint.

Dressed in garlands, the couple face either side of a silk screen held by the priests of both families. Guests sing songs and toss rice. When the priests remove the screen, the couple exchange garlands. A sacred fire is lit and the couple pour *ghee*, or clarified butter, onto it as they pray for wealth, healthy children, and long life. Then they circle the fire seven times to symbolize longevity, prosperity, and happiness.

The last Hindu rite comes after death. Hindus believe that death traps the soul in the skull. Only sacred fire can release it to take its next form. To ensure that a person's soul is released, the deceased is cremated in a fire arranged to direct most of its heat at the skull. Before the funeral pyre is lit, the eldest male relative of the deceased circles the fire several times. He lights the fire, and priests chant from sacred texts. The ritual continues until the skull breaks, and the mourners leave. After three days, the ashes are scattered into a holy river.

Buddhist Rituals

In contrast to Hinduism, Buddhism has fewer rites. The main Buddhist celebration is Buddha Purnima. This holiday commemorates the Buddha's birth, death, and enlightenment. During the rest of the year, observant Buddhists "take refuge in the three jewels." These are the Buddha, his teachings, and his followers. Buddhists recognize the importance of birth, puberty, and marriage, but do not celebrate them with rituals. They mourn death with simple acts. After a death, family members offer charity to the monks. The merit of this act transfers to the deceased.

This girl from Gujarat *(left)* is festooning a wall with handprints and animals during Diwali. The tradition is called Rangoli, which is the art of decorating. White stone, lime, and rice flour are some of the materials used to draw Rangoli designs. A monk *(above)* kneels before the reclining Buddha statue at the Mahaparinirvana Stupa in Kushinagar, one of the holiest Buddhist temples in India. Kushinagar is a major pilgrimage site for Buddhist monks, as it was here that Gautama Buddha died at age eighty after reaching enlightenment, or *mahaparinirvana*.

To become a Buddhist, a person informally recites the three refuges and the five precepts, which are as follows: refrain from killing; refrain from stealing; refrain from lying, slandering, gossiping, and spreading rumors; refrain from sexual misconduct; and refrain from taking intoxicants. The decision to become a Buddhist is a personal one and does does not depend upon the approval of Buddhist monks.

The most important Buddhist rites address the transition from the previous life of home and family to the new life of a homeless monk. These ceremonies are ritual re-enactments of Siddhartha Gautama's own progress to enlightenment. Every Buddhist monk must reject worldly ties and possessions just as Gautama did.

Boys as young as eight can join the Buddhist order as novices. They change their names, shave their heads, and dress in traditional saffron robes. After age twenty, they become full monks.

Muslim Rituals

The most important Muslim holiday is Ramadan. Ramadan is not a festival, but a month of fasting. It commemorates the appearance of the angel Gabriel and the revelation of the Koran to the prophet Muhammad. During this month, observant

Muslims fast from sunrise to sunset and occupy themselves with quiet prayer. At the end of Ramadan, they break their fasts at the celebration of Ramadan-Id or Id-ul-Fitr.

Like Hindus, Muslims perform numerous life rituals. When a baby is born, Muslims whisper the call to prayer into his or her ear. Seven days later, they perform the *aqiqah* ceremony. This gives the child a name.

At the age of four, Muslim children take part in the *bismillah* ceremony. The Muslim child recites "In the name of God the Compassionate and the

Muslims traditionally pray five times a day, either at home or at the mosque. Muslims fast each day until sundown during the month of Ramadan to focus on spiritual rather than material matters.

Merciful," which begins the Muslim education. For boys, there is another ceremony between the ages of seven and twelve when they are circumcised.

Nikah, or marriage, is a social ritual, not a sacrament. It is a legal contract between two people, but a devout marriage is an act of obedience to God.

In countries where it is legal, Muslim men may marry as many as four wives. If they do so, they must treat each wife equally. Women, however, may marry only one man. Traditionally, a man could divorce a wife by repeating the phrase "I divorce you" three times in a row, though this has no basis in Islamic teachings.

These Parsis are believers in Zoroastrianism, one of the oldest monotheistic religions in the world. The Navjote ceremony pictured here is the most important rite of passage in a Parsi child's life. A priest ties a sacred thread around the child's waist as he chants the Ahuna-Vairya, verses that contain the fundamental doctrines of Zoroastrianism.

Before death, the Muslim's last words are a declaration of faith that ends with the name of God. The name of God was the first word whispered into the ear of the newborn Muslim and is the last sound from the lips of the dying Muslim. After death, the deceased is washed, covered, and taken to the mosque. The body is buried facing Mecca, the holy city of the Muslims.

THE RELIGIONS OF INDIA THROUGHOUT ITS HISTORY

6

I ndia is one of the world's major sources of religious ideas. Throughout history, it has produced Hinduism, Buddhism, Jainism, and Sikhism. Today, India has five major religions: Hinduism, Islam, Christianity, Jainism, and Sikhism. There are also small communities of Buddhists, Jews, and Zoroastrians.

Indian Religion and Thought

Hinduism is by far India's most widely practiced faith. It derives from the Vedism and Brahminism of the Aryan conquerors and includes such ideas as yoga, which may date back to Harappa.

In the 3,500 years since the Aryan invasion, only Islam has challenged Hindu dominance, influencing the region with its political power ever since. In the early years of Islam, there were only a few thousand Muslims in India. Today, Muslims comprise 13 to 15 percent of India's population, roughly equal to 15 percent of the world's Muslims.

During the British occupation of India, England's Protestant Christians won many religious converts, especially from among the lowest castes. This mass convergence of religion influenced social and political thought. Christ's rejection of vengeance and his emphasis on forgiveness, for instance, intrigued the nonviolent Hindu leader

This detail from the fifth-century Buddhist caves in Ajanta *(left)* shows the Buddha meditating while performing a variety of *mudras*, or hand postures. Created during the Gupta dynasty, the hand gestures are a visual vocabulary meant to symbolize the virtues of Buddhism, such as "Wheel of Dharma," which is the union of method and wisdom. Meditation upon these concepts while performing the mudra is thought to increase the practitioner's understanding. Making offerings to the gods, or *upachara (above)*, is a fundamental aspect of Hinduism. It is a way of welcoming the deities to Earth, an act of hospitality.

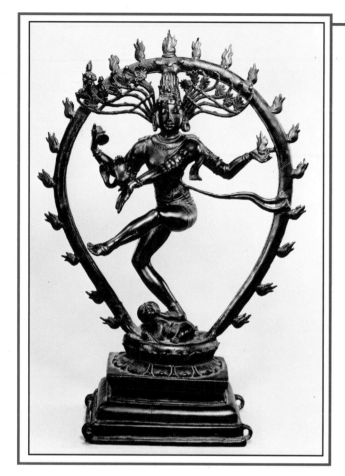

Shiva Nataraja is an eleventh-century sculpture from Madras. *Nataraja* means "lord of the dance," and *Shiva* embodies the movement of the universe. Hindus believe that if he stops dancing, the universe will end. He is surrounded by fire, a symbol of life and death. One leg is lifted to symbolize liberation, while the other is crushing a demon.

Mohandas Gandhi. Later, Gandhi's ideas of nonviolent resistance influenced the United States's Christian reverend Dr. Martin Luther King Jr.

Hinduism

The word "Hindu," derived from "Indus," once described native Indians who did not practice such religions as Islam, Christianity, or Judaism, or the less popular Indian religions of Buddhism, Jainism, or Sikhism. There is no organized Hindu church. Instead, there are shared ideas that date to the Vedas or earlier.

Hindus worship Parabrahma, or the Supreme Universal Soul. This soul has three selves: Brahma, the Creator; Vishnu, the Preserver; and Shiva, the Destroyer. Together they become the ultimate god known as Brahman, which should not be confused with the priestly caste known as Brahmin. They symbolize birth, life, and death. Brahma creates the world and fills it with people. Vishnu preserves and oversees it. Time passes and people neglect their duties. They lose caste. Their *dharma*, or dutifulness, shrinks to half. Then it shrinks again. The world is in chaos. This period is Kaliyuga. (According to Hindu mythology, the world is currently in this stage.) Finally, Shiva incinerates the world with his fiery third eye of destruction. Then Brahma re-creates it.

In statues and paintings, Brahma, Vishnu, and Shiva each have four arms. Brahma, in his all-seeing wisdom, also has four heads. The four sacred Vedas came

This painting from Uttar Pradesh is a contemporary example of one way that Hindus celebrate Krishna in Hinduism. Krishna is considered an incarnation of the god Vishnu, sustainer of the universe. Legends reveal that women flock to Krishna because of his bravery. The blue hue of Krishna's skin is attributed to such qualities as heroism, mental stability, and depth of character.

from his four mouths. He is married to Saraswati, the goddess of knowledge, who rides a swan. Brahma's own steed, the sea turtle, can be seen in a shrine at Pushkar. Beyond this, there are few temples to Brahma. Most Hindus are either Shaivas (worshipers of Shiva) or Vaishnaivas (worshipers of Vishnu).

As the world's preserver, Vishnu has lived on the earth nine times in nine different incarnations. For the first six, he was a fish, a tortoise, a boar, a half-man, a beggar-dwarf, and Parsurama, the ax-wielder. In his seventh life, as the hero Rama, he destroyed the demon king Ravana. Vishnu's eighth life was that of the blue-skinned cowherd Krishna. As Krishna, he advised the Pandava hero Arjuna in his war against the Kauravas. He also rescued the milk-maids from the demon king Naraka and married all of them. Famous for his 16,000 girlfriends, Krishna's dearest love was Radha. Their romance represents both romantic happiness and the bond between humans and gods. Next, Vishnu returned as the Buddha, perhaps to regain the devotion of those Hindus who strayed from him to

A sadhu sits on the ground and worships in Varanasi, a city of pilgrimage for the devout in Uttar Pradesh. It is considered sacred because of its proximity to the Ganges River and is the dwelling place of the deity Shiva.

Buddhism. According to Hindu belief, he will appear once more on Earth as the horse-headed Kalki. In heaven, he is married to Lakshmi, the goddess of good fortune.

Shiva the Destroyer, symbolized by the deadly cobra, once arrived home to find his adored wife, Parvati, talking to a man. Instantly, he cut off the man's head. Parvati explained that the man was their son, born in Shiva's absence. Horrified, Shiva grabbed the head of the first creature he could find to replace it. The son became the elephant-headed god, Ganesh. Parvati is also Kali, the goddess of destruction and carrier of disease and misery.

Besides the major gods, there are an endless variety of lesser gods. These include Hanuman, the monkey god who helped Rama, and Kartikeya, the six-headed god of war.

In addition to myths, Hindus share ideas about human existence. Hindu thought describes four human goals: achievement of wealth, or *purushartha*; satisfaction of desire, or *kama*; performance of duty, or *dharma*; and freedom from the cycle of death and rebirth, or *moksha*. Within each life, a person goes through the four phases of student (*brahmacharya*); then parent (*grihastha*); retired thinker (*vanaprastha*); and, finally, wandering ascetic (*sanyasa*), supported by alms, or charity.

The Roots of Hinduism

Modern Hinduism descends from the Vedism of the Aryans. "Veda" means "knowledge" or "wisdom." Vedism is mystic, which means it strives for direct union with God. For the Indians, this meant fusing the individual soul, the *atma*, with the world soul, the Brahman. The four sacred Vedas explained how to reach this state. In time, Vedism became Brahminism, which later became Hinduism.

This Buddhist monk is creating prayer flags in the Rumtek monastery in Sikkim, India. Prayer flags are inscribed with Buddhist symbols, prayers, and mantras, and may be hung outside the home or place of worship to spread messages of faith and hope.

The major Vedic god was the war god Indra. Armed with thunderbolts, he destroyed the serpent Vritra, the force of destruction. Most of the other Vedic deities are forces of nature. Surya, Dyaus, Savitri, and Aditya are sun gods. Usha is the goddess of the dawn, Vayu is the wind god, Agni is the fire god, and Soma is the god of the mind-altering *soma* plant.

Vedism divides the world into religion, war and law, and fertility. In the Rig Veda, the first Veda, the god Purusha is dismembered. His head became the Brahmins, his arms became the Kshatriyas, his loins became the Vaisyas, and his feet became the Shudras. Physical reality exists on a series of plains. The highest is heaven, where the gods of religion and order live. Indra and his stormy warrior gods live in the atmosphere. Below them, on Earth, humans live with animals, plants, and fire. Demons inhabit the underworld.

The main ritual of Vedic worship was sacrifice. Worshipers sacrificed butter, cakes, or animals into fire. A successful sacrifice pleased the gods and brought health, wealth, or victory. A person who made enough sacrifices secured his or her place in heaven.

As Vedism evolved, it changed to include reincarnation. After death, instead of going to heaven, people were born again. Whether the new life was better or worse depended upon behavior in the previous life. This was karma. A person who lived enough pure and holy lives would be freed from the cycle and become one with Brahman, the world soul.

The purest and holiest people were ascetics. Asceticism is self-denial. The ascetic fasts and meditates. Vedic sacrifice, which was external, had changed to the personal sacrifice of asceticism, which is internal. One ascetic practice was yoga. Yoga links a person's physical and spiritual selves. It is a direct route to holiness.

As the religion continued to change, the Vedas became less relevant. The Brahmins added the Brahmanas and the Upanishads. In the first century AD,

Pictured here next to a sculpture of the Buddha is a *bodhi* tree, considered sacred to Buddhists. After seven years of soul searching, Gautama, a Nepali prince, went to Bodhgaya in northern India and decided to sit under the *bodhi* tree until he reached enlightenment. He spent many days and nights in meditation near the tree when he finally achieved inner peace.

the Brahmins wrote the Vedanta, or "the end of the Vedas." This text includes the Brahma Sutras, which are the official root of modern Hinduism.

Buddhism

Until the seventh century AD, when its ideas began to blend with dominant Hindu ideas, Buddhism was a major religion in India. Today, much of Nepal and Sri Lanka are Buddhist, as well as parts of China, Japan, Korea, Thailand, and Cambodia.

Buddhists follow the teachings of a Kshatriya prince named Siddhartha Gautama (563–483 BC). Gautama was born in Kapilavastu in northern India. He died in Kushinagara (Nepal) at the age of eighty. At twenty-nine, Gautama gave up his life for a spiritual existence.

Though he practiced yoga and radical asceticism for several years, he did not reach enlightenment. Next, he tried meditation. In 528 BC, at Bodhgaya (in modern Bihar), he reached enlightenment. His followers called him the Buddha, which means "the enlightened one."

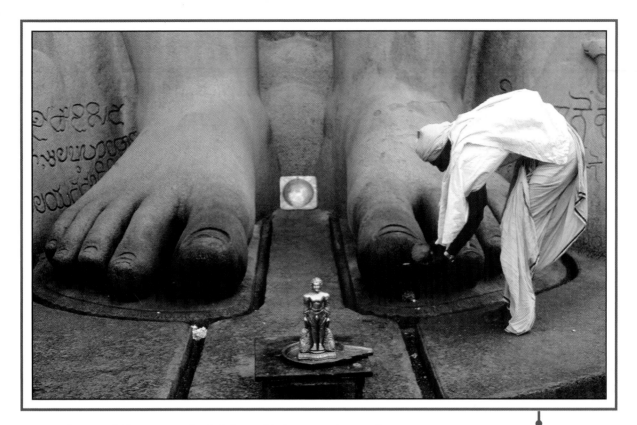

The Buddha preached his enlightenment and composed the Four Noble Truths: Life is suffering; suffering is caused by desire; to end suffering, one must overcome desire. To overcome desire, one must forsake the illusions of the senses. To live by these truths, one must follow the Buddha's Eightfold Path of right knowledge, right purpose, right speech, right action, right occupation, right effort, self-mastery, and right meditation.

The Buddha was a radical religious figure. He rejected the absolute authority of the Brahmin priests. In Buddhism, there was no sacrifice and no caste system. Buddhists believe in avoiding harm to oneself or others. More important, they seek detachment from desire. An enlightened person is loving, kind, compassionate, and serene. At the end of the Buddha's Eightfold Path, there is a final state of ultimate stillness. It is a void outside and beyond the noise and chaos of human suffering. The ultimate state of blessedness is *nirvana*, or the extinction of the self.

A Jain (a follower of Jainism) makes devotions to the colossal Gommateshwara Statue at the Shravanabelagola Temple, in southern India. One of the tallest statues in the world, Gommateshwara was carved in AD 981. Every twelve years, Jains flock to Shravanabelagola to attend the Mahamastakabhisheka Festival, where they anoint the giant figure with pots of milk, coconut, and bananas.

These Sikhs live in the Punjab region, near Pakistan. They are wearing turbans, which are a symbol of holiness in the Sikh religion. Sikhs consider the hair to be sacred. They often grow their hair, but they must cover it. Exchanging turbans with a Sikh is considered a sign of a permanent friendship.

Jainism

Jainism is a non-Vedic Indian faith and major world religion. Jains believe in the sacredness of all life. Their primary tenet is *ahimsa*, or nonviolence. According to Jainist doctrine, every particle in the universe has a soul. All Jains are vegetarians, and strict Jains wear fine mesh masks to avoid accidentally inhaling—and killing—tiny insects. They carry brooms to sweep any invisible creatures out of the way of their feet as they walk.

Sikhism

Founded by Guru Nanak (1469–1539) to bridge the conflict between Hinduism and Islam, Sikhism is not an offshoot of either, but a "third force." Nanak was born into a Hindu family in a village west of Lahore. Until 1500, he worked for a Muslim nobleman. Then he had a religious experience. Afterward, he declared: "There is no real Hindu and no real Muslim."

Having realized this, Nanak began to wander the countryside. He met and spoke with religious leaders. Their ideas inspired him to shape Sikhism.

Nanak preached loving devotion to a god who did not assume a human form. Worshipers focused on "God's name, charity, and bathing." Nanak taught his followers that it was important to live righteously in the world. It was equally important to meditate and pray. Today, Sikhs still follow the teachings of Nanak.

Islam

Islam, the religion of the Muslims, is native to the Middle East. Like Christianity and Judaism, it is monotheistic, which means Muslims worship one god, Allah. Allah spoke to the Islamic prophet Muhammad 1,400 years ago. His teachings, which include precise rules for modern life, are recorded in a holy book called the Koran.

This Muslim studies the Koran at the Jama Masjid (mosque) in Old Delhi. Muslims have a rich history in India that spans almost 1,300 years. Islam differs fundamentally from Hinduism in that Muslims worship only one god. Islam places ultimate importance on the teachings of its holy book, the Koran.

The obligations of a Muslim include prayer, charity, fasting, and the *hajj*, or pilgrimage to the holy city of Mecca in Saudi Arabia. Mecca was the birthplace of Muhammad, in AD 571. All Muslims must attempt the hajj once in their lives if they are able. Five times a day—upon waking, at noon, at mid-afternoon, at sunset, and before retiring—Muslims pray facing the direction of Mecca. They observe certain dietary restrictions, and many Muslim women cover their hair.

The differences between Hinduism and Islam are significant. Hinduism derives from an ancient intellectual and mythic tradition. Islam is much younger and has a single holy scripture. Hinduism includes countless regional variations, but Islam has only two major sects, the Sunnis and Shi'ites. Hindu religious art includes elaborate and sometimes highly fantastic portraits of its gods. In Islam, it is sacrilegious to represent the face of God. Muslims decorate their mosques with elaborate geometrical patterns and stylized script that re-creates text from the Koran.

Islam entered India when Muhammad bin Qasim invaded Sind, at the Indus River Delta, in AD 711. The Muslims took many Hindu captives. Islamic law offered non-believers conversion or death. The few Muslims ruling northwestern India could not possibly kill or convert every one of the hundreds of thousands of new subjects. They solved the problem by calling the Indians *dhimmi*.

"Dhimmi" means "people of the book." Groups mentioned in the Koran, like Jews and Christians, are dhimmi. The Indians were not mentioned in the Koran, but calling them dhimmi gave the Muslims a reason not to kill them. This willingness to change rigid rules eased the Muslim entrance into India.

By the twelfth century, the Muslim population in India was growing. In the sixteenth century, during the reign of the Mughal king Akbar (1556–1605), Islam became a dominant religion in western Punjab and eastern Bengal. Akbar's capital was in the north. In the south, Islam struggled to pass the Deccan Plateau. The Muslim population rose only in growing cities.

By the eighteenth and nineteenth centuries, Indian Islam had incorporated many Hindu ideas and practices into its faith, resulting in devotional cults like that of Sufism. By the nineteenth century, Muslim political power had waned in northern India. While tensions between Hindus, Muslims, and Sikhs have always existed in India, most of the followers of each faith continue to live in harmony. However, Partition and the creation of Muslim Pakistan sometimes resulted in bitter clashes between Hindus and Muslims.

Zoroastrianism

Another Middle Eastern import, Zoroastrianism is the oldest prophetic religion. It is based on the teachings of the prophet Zarathushtra, or Zoroaster, from an area that is now northeast Iran. From the sixth century BC until the seventh century AD, Zoroastrianism was the state religion of a territory that reached from northern India to Anatolia (part of Turkey).

In the seventh century, the Arabs invaded Persia (Iran) and drove the Zoroastrians into the desert, establishing Islam as Persia's primary religion. In 936, a small group of Zoroastrians settled on India's northwest coast near modern Bombay (Mumbai). They became known as Parsis, which comes from the word "Persians." Today, India is home to most of the world's Zoroastrians.

Christianity

In the sixth century, the Nestorian Church sent Christian missionaries to Kerala. These Christians claim St. Thomas the Apostle as their founder. They are called Thomas Syrian Christians and believe that St. Thomas was martyred in Tamil Nadu and buried at Mailapur. Originally from Syria, this Christian sect absorbed some Hindu ideas. Its members had a high social status and did not interact with members of low castes.

In 1557, during the Mughal Empire, Portuguese missionaries founded an archbishopric at Goa to train Indians as priests. Jesuit missionaries visited the court of Akbar. In the seventeenth century, the Roman Catholic Church tried to bring India's Syrian Christians into the Catholic fold. The Catholics insisted that good Christians visit the sick or dying. To the horror of the Syrian Christians, this meant visiting members of low castes, an idea that made many Indians uncomfortable. Some left the church in protest.

Christian churches eventually solved this problem by training low-caste priests. Under the British, Protestant missionaries from Anglican, Lutheran, and Methodist churches preached, taught, and healed members of every caste. Today, Christianity is a small minority of approximately 14 million Indians.

Judaism

The Jewish population in India is ancient. Jewish communities in the region date back to the thirteenth century. Modern Jews have settled on the Konkan coast near Mumbai and in Cochin.

There have been several surges in India's Jewish population. In the early years of the European East India Companies, Jewish traders moved to India to work in company offices. During World War II, a wave of refugees arrived from countries threatened by Nazi Germany.

India's Jewish population was largest in the last days of the British raj. In 1947, there were more than 25,000 Jews living in India. Now that number is closer to a few thousand.

THE ART AND ARCHITECTURE OF INDIA

7

Indian art is rich and diverse. Over a few thousand years, India has produced the densely carved Hindu temples of the Dravidians, the unearthly severity of the Muslim Taj Mahal, the calm immensity of Buddhist sculpture, and the crisp jewel-tones of Rajput painting.

Ancient Art

Ancient Indian art is commonly divided into several major periods. The earliest works are central Indian rock paintings from 5500 BC. Most depict hunting scenes. The next period is the Indus River Valley culture of 2000 BC. The art that survives from this period includes square white seals of animals and pictographs from Harappa. The sophisticated art of the Aryan invaders was primarily ornate wooden carvings and palace wall paintings, most of which have been destroyed by time.

Early Buddhist Art

In 326 BC, Alexander the Great reached the kingdom of a Gandharan ally in the northwest corner of India. He traveled with soldiers, politicians, traders, and sculptors. The Buddhist artists of Gandhara admired the Greek sculptors' skills. They adopted the Greek style of carving human torsos in thinly draped fabrics. A typical Gandharan sculpture of this period shows the Buddha's robe as a series of

The Charminar in Hyderabad *(left)* was built in 1591 by Quli Qutub Shah and is from the Qutub Shahi dynasty. This archway is often referred to as the Arc de Triomphe of the East. The mosque consists of four minarets, forty-five prayer rooms, and a courtyard. Its style is referred to as Indo-Sarcenic, which is a blend of Hindu and Muslim traditions. This four-lion capital *(above)* once stood atop an Asokan pillar and is from the Mauryan dynasty (322–185 BC). Asoka erected the pillar where Buddha proclaimed his philosophy of enlightenment. The four lions are meant to represent power, courage, and confidence. The pillar is now the national emblem of India.

This representation of the Bodhisattva Maitreya was sculpted in the Gandharan style and represents the Buddha of the Future, who will one day return to Earth as a secular being to save mankind.

lines running diagonally across his chest from one shoulder, much like a Greek work of the era. Based on the Greek toga, this use of fabric inspired the *saris* and *dhotis* of India.

Greek influence in Indian art soon waned and was followed by the Mauryas, whose art was grander and more sophisticated. The third Mauryan emperor was Asoka. Asoka placed pillars—some as tall as thirty-two feet (ten meters), carved with edicts (laws)—at the edges of his empire. The best preserved of these is at Lauriya Nandangar. It is a solid column of polished sandstone, topped by a seated lion. The fineness of the carving is as impressive as the engineering skill that erected the fifty-ton column.

Very few figural sculptures remain from this era. One of the best is a freestanding figure of a *yakshi*, or female earth spirit. The life-sized sandstone statue gleams with the glossy polish of Mauryan work. Its full curves give the hard stone a fleshlike softness emphasized by details of jewelry and dress. Some of the period's most beautiful stone carvings can still be seen at Sarnath and Sanchi, in Madhya Pradesh.

After Asoka, the Mauryan Empire split apart. The tribal Andhras took power in the Deccan. By the second century AD, they controlled central India from coast to coast. At the end of the first century AD, they reached

This fourth-century AD schist relief sculpture from the Gandharan era is known as *The Descent of the Buddha*. The fragment illustrates the moment when Buddha descended back to Earth after having spent time in heaven with his deceased mother.

The Qutab Minar in Delhi was completed during the reign of Emperor Firoz Shah Tughlaq in 1368. The surrounding complex is believed to have originally been a Hindu temple that was later converted into a mosque. It represents the Islamic conquest in India.

Sanchi. Their renovation of a Sanchi *stupa,* or Buddhist monastery, became the greatest Buddhist monument in India. It was a dome sixty feet (twenty meters) across and twenty-five feet (eight meters) high in a square space surrounded by a railing. The Andhras hired local ivory workers to decorate four stone gates for the temple. The delicate ivory techniques created unusually graceful stone carvings. Among these, several yakshi mark a dramatic advance in Indian sculpture. They are lightly poised and appear effortlessly alive. Each is in the three-body-bends pose *(tribhanga)* that became standard in Indian sculpture.

The Classical Period

In AD 320, the Gupta Empire began India's classical art period. The Gupta court encouraged all forms of art and learning, and the period is often referred to as one of Indian renaissance. Gupta sculpture is famous for its careful detail, liquid sensuality, and Buddhist tranquillity. During this period, the Buddha's clothes and physical position reached perfection. Many modern images of the Buddha use a style

The Great Stupa at Sanchi is one of the most important Buddhist monuments in India and consists of burial mounds that were constructed from the third century BC to the twelfth century AD. Visitors to the Great Stupa observe its hemispherical shape, which represents the heaven that covers Earth and its alignment with the four points of the compass. Pilgrims complete a circumnavigation of the dome as an act of devotion.

Pictured here is the rock sculpture *Arjuna's Penance*, also known as *The Descent of the Ganges*. Carved from a single boulder in AD 640, it represents the Ganges River flowing from heaven to Earth and giving all creatures the gift of life.

that reflects the Gupta period. India's earliest surviving paintings also date from this time.

As the Guptas perfected the serenity of Buddhist art, the Dravidians of southern India developed a more sculpturally complex Hindu art. They worked in both stone and bronze. The Pallavas had succeeded the Andhras and ruled most of the peninsula. The Pallavas were a seafaring people. Some of their greatest works are the cave temples and open-air reliefs carved into the granite ridges along the seaport at Mamallapuram (present-day Mahabalipuram). The most dramatic relief sculpture is more than twenty feet high (six meters) and eighty feet (twenty-six meters) long. It depicts more than a hundred figures of gods, people, and animals.

The Mamallapuram relief tells the story of the descent to Earth of the sacred Ganges River. For 1,000 years, an ascetic named Bhagiratha denied himself food, water, and companionship in order to focus his whole being on spiritual purity. Impressed, the gods granted him one wish. Bhagiratha asked that the heavenly Ganges River flow from heaven to Earth, so humans could enjoy its fertile blessings. The gods agreed, but as they prepared to release the water, they worried that the force of its fall would destroy Earth. Shiva volunteered to soften the blow with his head. The river water crashed into his hair, meandered through his tangled locks for several eons, and finally flowed gently onto Earth.

The carving at Mamallapuram shows the moment when the water reached Earth. In its center, the serpent king and queen swim up through the river around gods, humans, and animals. On the right side of the river cleft, the smooth, dense shape of an enormous elephant balances a complex composition of smaller creatures on the left. During ceremonies and festivals, water flows down through the carving. This ritual re-creates the moment of the Ganges' arrival on Earth.

The Medieval Period

The medieval period of Indian art dates from the eighth century, when the Muslims arrived in the Indus Delta, to the thirteenth century, when Islam dominated north India. Throughout the five centuries, Buddhist and Hindu art flourished. In pre-Islamic Hindu art, sculpture and architecture were fused. Surfaces were often carved with gods, beasts, and sacred symbols. After the arrival of Islam, northern Hindu works started to show a strong Persian influence and the influence of Buddhism faded out of northern India altogether.

During the medieval period, Hindu temple architecture developed an unusual bee-hive shape called the *rekha*. Builders curved the four sides of a tower gently inward as they reached the top. This soft taper gives Hindu temples a uniquely sensuous profile. Most are topped with flat, round, ribbed caps on which sit "vases of plenty." Medieval builders used little or no mortar to assemble these temples and depended on gravity to hold them together. Most decorative carving was done once the stones were in place.

A classic example of this Hindu style is the eleventh-century Mukteshvara Temple. Its sides are ribbed with deep vertical lines and its edges and entrances are dense with religious carvings. Another, the Surya Temple, or "Black Pagoda," stands on the beach of the Bay of Bengal at Konarak and was built in the

This thirteenth-century medieval temple was built in the rekha style and features a curved design. Known as the Kesava Temple, it is located in Mysore, India.

The Surya Temple of Konarak, also known as the "Black Pagoda," sits on the shores of the Bay of Bengal and is an example of medieval Indian temple architecture. It is built in the shape of the sun god Surya's chariot. The twenty-four wheels that surround it represent the hours of the day, and it is pulled by seven horses that represent the days of the week.

thirteenth century. Designed to represent the chariot of the sun god, sculptors carved twelve enormous wheels into its base and seven horses to run before it.

Unfortunately, many temples in northern India were demolished after the arrival of the Muslims in order to construct Islamic mosques, minarets, and tombs. These structures were built on Hindu sites. Many still stand today, such as the five-tier Qutb Minar and the Jama Masjid (Pearl Mosque), and are fine examples of Indo-Muslim architecture.

The Mughal Empire

The Islamic aesthetic was radically different from Hindu art. Mosque architects used abstract designs, colored stone, and elaborate inlay techniques rather than carving. The roots of Indian Islamic architecture lie in Syria and Persia. The mosques of these countries were ornamented with circular or fluted towers, detailed stonework, pointed arches, and cursive inscriptions from the Koran.

In India, the Muslim aesthetic began to change. Naturalistic Indian flowers soon surrounded the letters of Persia's cursive inlays. The marriage of Persian elegance and Indian naturalism is particularly clear in Mughal court painting. These lush scenes of courtly life show melancholy lovers in stormy landscapes and elegant aristocrats on dramatic hunts.

Some of the intense jewel tones in these works are actually from jewels. Painters sometimes ground their pigments from such semiprecious stones as malachite and lapis lazuli. They also used gold, silver, and a yellow dye called *peori* made from the urine of cows fed on mango leaves.

One of India's most stunning architectural achievements was built by the fifth Mughal emperor, Shah Jahan. Possibly the world's most beautiful building, the Taj

This Mughal miniature is a portrait of Arjumand Bano Begum, also known as Mumtaz Mahal. She was the wife of Emperor Shah Jahan and the inspiration for the Taj Mahal, which was built as her mausoleum. "The ivory gate through which all dreams pass" is how Rudyard Kipling described the monument, which is constructed almost entirely of white marble, allowing it to glow by sunlight and moonlight.

Mahal was a mausoleum for his beloved queen, Arjumand Bano Begum (also known as Mumtaz Mahal). The building is a faceted cube flanked by four slim minarets. Its central dome rises just above the minarets on a high drum, which gives the square shape a floating lightness. A long pool pairs the facade with its reflection. The otherworldly glow of the pure white marble surface is intensified by a delicate tracery of black stone and subtle floral inlay. It is most dramatic under the full moon or in the pink light of sunrise.

After the Mughals

Under the Muslims, the Hindus renewed past artistic styles and joined them with Islamic ideas. This work had the elegance of Islamic court art, yet it also featured aspects common to Indian works such as naturalism, spirituality, and eroticism. The finest Hindu painting from this period comes from such former Punjabi hill states as Rajasthan (Mewar), Jammu (Pahari), Basolhi, and Kangra.

The collapse of the Mughal Empire ended the period of Indian art uninfluenced by the West. When the Mughals fell to the British East India Company, the British wanted Indian art to reflect English tastes. Soon, Indian artists were producing landscape paintings in oil and watercolor. This movement toward the West in Indian art created the Company School. By the 1930s, the Bengali School returned to traditional Indian watercolor and developed a style that combined the tradition of Indian folk art with a Western influence. The British also left behind many works of architecture in India, including the

The artist Maqbool Fida Hussain was born in 1915 in Maharastra but moved to Bombay—now Mumbai—in 1937 to become a painter. He began his career painting movie billboards and designing toys. His personal work draws on Indian folk art and Hindu icons but employs an abstract, contemporary style.

Gateway of India in Mumbai and the palace of the viceroy in New Delhi, the residence of India's president.

Today, many modern Indian artists produce work that is rooted in Indian tradition but also recognizes Western influences. Some of India's most famous twentieth-century artists include Amrita Shergill, M. F. Hussain, and Krishen Khanna.

Crafts of India

India is famous for its bright saris, bronze water vessels, woven sandals, and glittering bangles. One of the most beautiful of Indian crafts is the brocade weaving of silk. Today, there are two major types of brocade: brocades of pure silk, or silk and cotton blends; and *zari* brocades woven with gold and silver. The silk used for the first type is usually Bengali *tanduri* or the delicate *banaka* used in turbans and handkerchiefs. The second uses the durable *mukta*, which can hold heavy gold patterns.

To make a brocade, raw silk is twisted—a process called silk throwing—and then reeled and checked for smoothness. Next it is bleached and degummed. (Raw silk is covered with a gumlike substance called sericin.) To remove it, weavers boil the silk in soapy water. This is a delicate procedure since boiling can weaken or damage silk fibers. When done correctly, boiling softens the silk and makes it easier to dye.

Dyeing silk is an art as well as a skill. A brocade's beautiful sheen depends on matching colors to please the eye and the heart. Red, the color of love, comes in three shades, or three states, of love. Yellow is spring, young blossoms, southern winds, and bees. Indigo, the color of Krishna's skin, makes one think of rain-filled clouds. Saffron, worn by Buddhist monks, is the color of the earth and

These silk dryers are working in Varanasi, a city known for its fine weaving. After the silk is unwound from the cocoon of the caterpillar, it is washed and then bleached to remove the gum on its surface. The thread is then placed in vats of hot dye before being rewashed and stretched for the final drying process.

the wandering yogi who renounces the world.

The most brilliant colors come from vegetable dyes. These produce vivid colors that last for decades. Today, aniline dyes are less expensive and widely available. Once the colors have been determined, weavers sketch the design, or *naksha*, of a brocade on paper. Next, they sew the finished naksha into a framework of cotton threads to make a guide.

In the past, designs varied from one century to another. In the Gupta period, popular nakshas included formal flowers, birds, and animals. Sixteenth-century Mughals favored Persian floral patterns. Under the raj, patterns mimicked the designs of British wallpapers.

Today, such ancient silk centers as Banaras, Ahmedabad, and Surat continue to weave very fine silk saris with lively color schemes. In the south, Kanchipuram and Tanjore produce gorgeous brocades heavily threaded with gold wire. For important occasions, like Indian marriages and festivals, colorful hand loomed fabrics remain a beautiful tradition.

A rural women in this photograph harvests silk cocoons. Silk is a product of the silkworm as it moves from the larval caterpillar stage of life to the pupal stage, encasing itself in a cocoon until it becomes a moth. Harvested cocoons are placed in a vat of boiling water to separate the cocoon from the larva, killing the caterpillar inside.

و دیو تنای جسرای را که طین برای نگاه بانی سینا که در شته بود از ترس این که خیند را او سینا

THE LITERATURE AND MUSIC OF INDIA

8

Much of India's early literature was composed orally, such as the Rig Veda, the first of the Vedas, and the great epic, the Mahabharata. Myths, legends, fables, and romances were told by storytellers rather than written in books. Few people could read, and paper was expensive. Telling stories was free, educational, and entertaining. It also demanded, and instilled, a good memory.

A memory aid in an oral story is called a mnemonic element. In the Mahabharata, the hero Arjuna is often called "the helmet-wearing Arjuna." Repeated phrases help storytellers maintain the flow of a tale. Rhythm also helps retention. This is why music makes song lyrics easy to remember. Other mnemonic methods included certain meters and structures. Early Indian verse written in the *shloka* or *anushtubh* meter had a memorable rhythm.

For centuries, the Rig Veda was told, retold, altered, and expanded. Finally, the Brahmins made a scholarly decision to set it down in writing. This written text allowed the Brahmins to study, teach, and edit their religious ideas. Unlike the Muslim Koran or the Christian Bible, the book that contains a Hindu sacred text is not holy. The act of speaking or chanting the text is holy.

Sanskrit

Brahmins in northern India committed the Vedas to paper in an early version of Sanskrit. In the north, Sanskrit was the language of priests and scholars.

This ink and watercolor folio *(left)* was taken from a late sixteenth-century Persian edition of the Ramayana. It is a part of the Freer Gallery of Art at the Smithsonian Institution in Washington, D.C. Hindus and Buddhists alike flock to Bodhgaya *(above)*, the place where Prince Gautama attained enlightenment. He taught the doctrines of Buddhism by word of mouth; no original Buddhist scriptures were written down. The first recorded canon of Buddhist literature is called the Tripitaka and was written in Sri Lanka in the Pali language during the first century BC.

This monk is studying a Buddhist scroll in the 500-year-old Thikse monastery in the Tibetan-Buddhist village of Ladakh, India. Formally known as the Kingdom of Ladakh, it is the home of the largest thriving Buddhist monastery in the entire Indus Valley.

(Southern Indians spoke Dravidian languages.) Later, the Brahmins added the Brahmanas to the Vedas. These stories were the beginning of narrative Indian text. Next came the Upanishads, which are "forest sittings" or "sessions with teachers." In these texts, priests and students discussed life and the relationship between humans and gods.

By the fifth or sixth century BC, Buddhism and Jainism had influenced Brahminism's religious thinkers. This was the beginning of the blended Indian belief system that later became Hinduism. The new religion of Hinduism found expression in the Mahabharata and the Ramayana.

As Indian culture progressed, spoken language changed. Sanskrit speakers began to speak middle Indo-Aryan, although writers still used Sanskrit. The Mahabharata and the Ramayana were both written in Sanskrit, as were the great early texts of Buddhism, Jainism, and Hinduism. Major Indian poets, doctors, and astronomers wrote in Sanskrit.

Kalidasa was classical Sanskrit's greatest poet and playwright. During the fifth century AD, Kalidasa developed a style that was fresh and immediate, but also elegant. His portraits of court aristocrats held emotional feeling. He could convey the chaos of a summer storm or the slick, alert form of a cobra without sacrificing the elegance of court style. His major works include *Kumarasambhava* (Birth of the war god) and *Raghuvansha* (The dynasty of Raghu).

Muslim rule dealt a heavy blow to Sanskrit literature. Educated Muslims spoke and read Persian. Hindu writers lost their courtly audience for the language of Sanskrit. Eventually they wrote in Persian or other spoken languages.

Persian

As Muslim power grew, Persian literature came into favor. At first, native Persians dismissed the work of Persian-speaking Indians as uneducated. In time, Indo-Persian

Various Hindu religious and literary texts are featured in this photo. Included are the four Vedas (Rig Veda, Sama Veda, Yajur Veda, and Atharva Veda), which are printed in Sanskrit.

literature found its voice. By the thirteenth century, the Indo-Persian tradition had produced the Indian poet Amir Khusrau (1253–1325). Celebrated as "the parrot of India," Khusrau was considered a Persian master poet. Focusing on traditionally Persian themes, Khusrau wrote thousands of *masnavi* poems and romantic *ghazal* love poems.

Hindi

Khusrau also wrote Indian-language or Hindustani verse. Southeast of Punjab, the non-Muslim poetic tradition dates to the eleventh century. This includes the heroic tales of the Rajasthani poets.

One popular Hindustani form at this time was *bhakti*. Bhakti poems explored religious ideas. Ram-bhakti described Rama as an incarnation of Vishnu. The most famous poet of Ram-bhakti was Tulsidas (1532–1623), considered the greatest poet of his time. His *Ramcharitmanas* is an adaptation of the Ramayana. It describes Rama's victory over Ravana and includes spiritual teachings. Some people call it the "Bible of Northern India."

By the seventeenth century, fewer and fewer people spoke Persian. Most Hindus in the country spoke Hindustani dialects. Muslims spoke a version of Hindustani called Urdu. In the far south, people still spoke Dravidian languages. By the end of the Mughal Empire, people spoke Persian only at court. The court poets of this period developed a brilliant, artificial style called the "Indian style." It was the last phase in India for a language that was quickly dying.

When the British took power from the Mughals, they tried to use Persian to govern. Since barely anyone spoke it, however, it was a poor choice. In 1835, the British abolished the official use of Persian, but not everyone abandoned it completely. The great Urdu poet Mirza Asadullah Ghalib (1797–1869) wrote an Indo-Persian prose

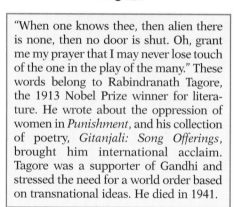

memoir titled *Dastanbu*. In it, he did not use a single Arabic word. It remains one of the purest manifestations of Indo-Persian writing. During this period, Hindustani dialects evolved and improved literacy dramatically.

English

Eventually, the British raj made English the language of politics and education. Indian writers who wrote in English already had a Western audience. Many addressed social, political, and economic issues. Gandhi, Rabindranath Tagore, and Jawaharlal Nehru each used English to write books and articles on India. Tagore's work in several languages won him the 1913 Nobel Prize for literature.

As writing in English flourished, Indian writers questioned its cost to the tradition of Indian literature. Many modern Indian writers, like Salman Rushdie, Anita Desai, and Ruth Prawer Jhabvala, write English-language works that explore the issues of Westernized Indians.

Partition created another layer of complication. Pakistan uses and teaches English less than India. There is very little Pakistani writing in English. Most of the best contemporary Pakistani writers who use English live abroad, like Bapsi Sidhwa and Zulfikar Ghose.

"When one knows thee, then alien there is none, then no door is shut. Oh, grant me my prayer that I may never lose touch of the one in the play of the many." These words belong to Rabindranath Tagore, the 1913 Nobel Prize winner for literature. He wrote about the oppression of women in *Punishment*, and his collection of poetry, *Gitanjali: Song Offerings*, brought him international acclaim. Tagore was a supporter of Gandhi and stressed the need for a world order based on transnational ideas. He died in 1941.

Classical Music

Classical Indian music comes directly from the Brahmin chanting of the Rig Veda. The Brahmins believed that making music was necessary to the order of the universe. This order hinged on the will of the gods and the behavior of humans, including worship and performance.

Classical Indian music has two basic elements: the *tala*, or rhythm, which sets the number of beats, and the *raga*, or melody. The first formal discussion of music appears in the *Natyashastra*. Written in the third or fourth century AD, this work divided musical instruments into wind, string, and percussion instruments. In the eighth or ninth

century, another text, the *Brihaddesi*, defined ragas. The thirteenth-century *Sangitratnakara* described the history and state of music.

In the early thirteenth century, under the Delhi sultanate, there were two styles of Indian music: Persian-influenced Hindustani music, played in northern India, and melodic Karnatak music, which dominated the south. The styles were similar but distinct. Both combined vocal or instrumental soloists with a drummer for rhythm and a *tanpura* player to provide a "drone." Each had its own traditions and performers.

A traditional Hindustani performance starts with a set composition. Then, the players improvise. These improvisations always return to the original composition, but, for periods, they can move away from it entirely. The major stringed instruments are the *sitar* and the *sarod*. These are both long-necked, multi-stringed, small-bodied members of the guitar family. Hindustani music also uses the *sarangi*, which uses a bow like a violin. A wind instrument, the *shahnai*, is like an oboe. For percussion, there are two drums, the twin *tabla*, which is like a bongo, and the *pakhavaj*.

Karnatak music is less improvisational. It places more stress on the original composition. To this, it adds memorized variations. The major strings in a Karnatak

Musicians Ustad Alla Rakha and Ustad Zakir Hussain are pictured here performing a tabla duet. The tabla is a type of drum tuned to specific pitches and played to emphasize both tone and rhythm. It first became popular in the eighteenth century.

performance are the *vina*, which rests on the floor, and the violin. The wind instrument is the flute. In some cases, Karnatak performances use a type of oboe called a *nagasvaram* and a drum called a *tavil*.

Modern Music

Today's Indian musicians experiment with instruments from all over the world. Southern performances include saxophones, clarinets, and mandolins. Northern performers are fond of the slide guitar. Modern technology has also made music more widely available. In the old days, refined musical performance was only for the wealthy. Now, recordings and radio have increased India's listening audience to millions.

The music of the public is folk music. Women still sing to soothe the smallpox goddess. Laborers sing to give rhythm to their work. Everyone sings at celebrations. Just as the music of high culture is free to everyone over the radio, regional music now reaches listeners all over the country.

Dance

The ancient Sanskrit word for music, *sangita*, included dance and drama. India's musical tradition is deeply linked to dance. And dance, as a form of worship, is closely tied to religion.

Two women perform a traditional Bharatanatyam dance outside a temple in Bhubaneswar, Orissa Province. Bharatanatyam originates with the *devadasis*, or dancing girls, who performed the dance at Tamil shrines. Bharatanatyam is meant to evoke the concept of *sringara bhakti*, or worship through love.

Indian artists, whether of dance, music, or craft, are only initiated into their field by a close relationship with a master teacher, or guru.

According to Hindu tradition, Shiva created dance. As *Nataraja*, the Lord of the Dance, Shiva performed the *tandava*, or cosmic dance.

Like music, dance is regional. There are several ancient dance forms, each of which evolved in a different section of India. The oldest is the woman's dance, *bharat natyam*, of Tamil Nadu. For centuries, it was performed by *devadasis*, young Dravidian priestesses. Accompanied by musicians, a solo female performer begins with a sensual *alarippu*. She punctuates her *nritya*, or pure dance, with facial expressions, hand movements, and the chime of ankle bracelets. The *odissi* of Orissa is similarly devout in spirit.

Kathakali, which means "dance-drama," is one of India's most famous dance forms. It grew from a physically grueling form of yoga. Performances are narrative and dramatic. They illustrate the battles and love affairs of gods and warriors. Kathakali dancers are all men. They perform the works in elaborate costumes, masks, and dramatic makeup. An equally beautiful and elaborate dance-drama is the *kuchipudi* of southern Andhara Pradesh.

Northern Indian *kathak* is fast, energetic, and complex. Related to Persian dance, it is athletic and sensual. In the Mughal court, kathak was often performed by *nautch* girls, or dancing courtesans.

Beyond these are thousands of regional folk forms, military marches, tribal dances, and martial arts forms. There are also dance rituals, performed to celebrate weddings or births or to frighten the demons of illness or drought.

Saswat Sen, trained by the legendary kathak dancer Birju Maharaj, performs at the Khajurahu Dance Festival. Kathak dancers wear bells on their ankles and step to the rhythm of the tabla drum. Dancers twirl around faster and faster until collapsing in a heap.

FAMOUS FOODS AND RECIPES OF INDIA

9

"An Indian is exposed to more combinations of flavors and seasonings than perhaps anyone else in the world. Our cuisine stretches from the freshness and sweetness of highly aromatic curry leaves to the dark pungency of the resin, **asafetida**, *whose earthy aroma tends to startle Westerners."*

—Madhur Jaffrey, *A Taste of India*

India's explosion of flavorful foods is derived from its combination of ingredients and cooking methods. A single spice can change a dish's flavor dramatically if its seeds are roasted, ground, or fried in hot oil in a process called *baghar*. Preparing spices correctly is crucial to Indian cooking. Grinding them can be exhausting, so cooks sometimes employ a professional spice grinder, or *masalchi*. After grinding nutmeg, mace, turmeric, cumin, fenugreek, ginger, fennel seeds, cardamom, cloves, cinnamon, and black pepper for a day's meal, the masalchi arranges them on a tray in tidy, colorful heaps.

The cook uses the spices from the masalchi's tray to flavor meat, fish, or vegetables. Next, fresh herbs, such as garlic, mint, basil, coriander, or thyme, give the dish additional flavor. A typical meal is surrounded with an array of condiments

This Rabari woman *(left)* is making *chapatis*, a type of unleavened Indian bread. Chapatis are made from wheat flour, vegetable oil, ghee (clarified butter), salt, and water. Chapatis are fried on a skillet or griddle, and then reheated for future meals. Because it isn't customary to use utensils in India, chapatis are often employed to scoop up food. The cuisine of India, such as the traditional food pictured above, is incredibly diverse. The basis of Indian cooking is the careful blending of spices. Each permutation of chili, turmeric, and a spectrum of other flavors give way to a unique blend. (Indians do not simply eat one main dish; there is always an array of breads, rice, *raitas*, and chutney to complement a meal. Chutney is a flavorful relish that is typically made from sour fruits. Raitas are yogurt sauces that cool spicy dishes.)

or "pickles." These range from the sweet topaz of mango chutney to the cool cream of minty yogurt *raita* to the grit of hot chili paste.

Indian food is regional. The food most Westerners eat in Indian restaurants is Punjabi. Before Indian independence, there were few fine restaurants in India because high-caste Hindus did not eat in public. After independence, restrictions relaxed. The Punjabis of northern India opened the first fine restaurants and served a "royal" cuisine. Still, some regional dishes are impossible to find outside private homes.

Indian recipes often relate to climate. Northern Kashmir is mountainous and cold. During the long winter season, people eat dried food. Strings of dehydrated fruits and vegetables hang from the ceilings of houses. Kashmiri cooks flavor dishes with warming spices like cinnamon. Tamil Nadu—the sultry tip of the Indian peninsula—is famous for its fiery spices. Southern cooks offset their spicy stews, like the chili-laced *sambhar*, with cool *raitas*. A breakfast favorite is steamed rice-cake *idlis* with coconut chutney.

All Indian food is served with bread or rice. Rice is more common in the south, where it grows easily in the moist climate. Cooks in other regions grind and steam wheat, barley, maize, or millet into pancakes. In the north, cooks favor wheat breads like *chapatis* and *parathas*. The oldest Indian baked breads are round and flat. When the Muslims arrived, they brought special clay ovens to cook the sweet leavened breads like puffed *naans* and *shirmals*, which are now common in the north.

Bread or rice is a utensil as well as a dish. Indians eat with the right hand (northerners with just the tips of the fingers) and use either a piece of bread or small mound of rice to scoop spoonfuls of meat or vegetables.

Drinks include tea or *chai*, south Indian coffee, the thirst-quenching lime *nimbu paani*, and refreshing yogurt *lassis*, which may be served sweet, plain, or salty.

Indian cuisine is rife with delicious snack food, and it's easy to find on any street corner. This photo shows a stack of *puri* for sale on the street in Rajasthan Province. Puri is a deep-fried bread made from wheat and rice flour.

Matar Paneer

Matar paneer, meaning peas and cheese, is a classic dish from the New Delhi area in northern India and is traditionally served with rice. (For this recipe, you can substitute tofu or cheddar cheese for paneer cheese.)

Cook Time: 30 min.
Serves: 4

1 large brick of paneer cheese
1 large package of frozen peas
1 onion
1 teaspoon pressed garlic
1 cup water
1 teaspoon ginger
1 tablespoon cumin
1 tablespoon coriander
1/2 teaspoon clove
1/4 teaspoon methi (fenugreek)
1 teaspoon salt
2 teaspoons flour (chickpea flour, besan)
enough water to make a paste
1 cup ground tomatoes or tomato puree
juice of 1 lemon

Cut one large brick of paneer cheese into cubes (tofu should be baked at 300 degrees in oven while you prepare the sauce). Thinly slice onion and sauté with pressed garlic in medium pan until brown. Add spices to onion/garlic at last minute of sauté. Stir until distributed. Add water. Mix flour and water paste. Add package of frozen peas to spice sauce and cook until hot. Dribble in chickpea/flour mixture while stirring. Sauce will thicken. Add tomatoes and lemon juice. Stir well. Add cheese or pre-heated tofu and simmer until it absorbs seasonings. Add water if necessary. Serve with rice.

This kaleidoscope of cookbooks attests to the many recipes available in Indian cooking. Hindu values such as vegetarianism explain the emphasis on grains and vegetables in Indian recipes. Muslim cuisine features dishes with lamb, goat, and chicken, but never pork, which is considered unclean. (Islamic beliefs also place an importance on the way meat is killed and prepared, called *halal*.)

These men are selling chili peppers and lemons, ingredients commonly featured in Hindu cooking, in a market in Old Delhi. These ingredients fall into two of the six categories of ayurvedic cuisine.

Hindu Cuisine

For Hindus, the main dietary restriction is beef. Typical meat dishes use fresh goat, though many Hindus are vegetarians. Those who are not, eat pork, poultry, and fish.

Hindu food is closely tied to religion. Food, or fasting, is a major part of holidays and festivals. Celebrations demand elaborate feasts. A lavish wedding feast is a good omen for a happy marriage. The delicious meal that celebrates a baby is a promise of that baby's strength. On the sad occasion of a funeral, people eat simple food, or they fast.

According to some Hindu thinkers, every substance, including food, has a force that is positive, negative, or neutral. The later stages of Hindu life are supposed to be spiritually pure. Some believe people in these stages should ingest only positive foods. The Indian writer and chef Madhur Jaffrey met with Swami Poornananda to explore this idea. Poornananda had created a test for the positivity or negativity of foods. Above a wide variety of food types, he suspended a *rudraksha* seed on a thread. If the seed swung in a clockwise direction, the food was positive. A counterclockwise motion meant the food was negative.

While Jaffrey watched, the rudraksha swung above nearly every food. Onions, salt, garlic, sugar, eggplant, tomatoes, and red chilies were negative. Ginger, honey, limes, almonds, apples, rice, and green chilies were positive. Potatoes were neutral and did not cause the rudraksha to swing at all.

Food can be medicinal as well as spiritual. Many follow India's ancient tradition of using food to improve health. Called *ayurveda*, this practice teaches how to balance phlegm, bile, and breath. This balance is *tridosha*. Hot, neutral, and mild foods will rebalance a body temperature disturbed by illness. A feverish person, for example, should eat cool yogurt-based foods to offset a fever's heat. People with colds should eat hot and spicy foods to warm themselves.

Sohan halwa is a delicious Indian treat, seen for sale at this Muslim market. The dessert is composed of sweet, milky syrup combined with flour, ghee, nuts, and cardamom. The mixture becomes solid when heated through and can be cut into bite-sized bits once cooled.

Muslim Foods and Feasts

The diets of Hindus and Muslims are very different. Muslims are far less likely to be vegetarians. They eat more meat in general and eat beef but not pork. Islamic dietary restrictions come from the Koran.

In the northwest, Muslim tastes have added Persian and Asian flavors to Indian cooking. Northern *mughlai* dishes include *rogan josh*, or curried lamb; *biryani*, which is chicken or lamb in saffron rice with rose water, almonds, and dried fruit; and *tandoori* meat or chicken, marinated in herbs roasted in a tandoor oven.

In Kashmir, a Muslim banquet, or *waazwaan*, is prepared by professional cooks called *waaza*. On the day of the feast, twenty or thirty waaza arrive at the home of the host.

The waaza slaughter animals in the Muslim manner. Then they cut them into seventy-two parts. Almost every part can be cooked. The finest parts are the livers, kidneys, and hearts. The cooks carry the meat into a large kitchen tent, cut it into cubes with cleavers, mince it, and pound it with mallets. After several hours, the meat is a smooth paste. The waaza form the paste into balls that they cook in spiced yogurt. They also roast chickens, braise rib chops in savory broth, and blend chutneys and raitas.

The artist M. F. Hussain is seen at a feast for the Muslim holiday Id-ul-Azha, which commemorates Abraham's willingness to sacrifice his son Isaac in the name of God. Abraham spared his son and sacrificed a ram instead, so Muslims typically slaughter a goat or sheep and share it among friends on this holiday.

DAILY LIFE AND CUSTOMS IN INDIA

10

When Hindus meet, they press their palms together, dip their heads, and say "Namaste," which is a common Indian greeting. Sikhs press their palms together and say "Sat sri akal," which means "God is great." Muslims touch the tips of their fingers to their foreheads and say "Salaam alaikum," or "Peace be unto you," or they exchange a soft handshake and bring their hands to their own hearts, a sign of sincerity. In urban areas, handshakes between both sexes have become more common, though Muslim women and men do not usually touch when they are introduced.

Indians traditionally do not touch strangers, even small children, on the head. The head is the holiest part of the body. Similarly, the sole of the foot is the dirtiest part of the body and should not be shown to another person. (To show respect to an elderly person, however, one might touch his or her feet.) The left hand is considered unclean and should not be used in any greetings or exchanges.

Indians are very hospitable. They invite people easily into their homes, treat them warmly, and feed them generously. When guests arrive, they usually leave their shoes at the door. This is also true at temples and mosques, where women cover their heads, legs, and arms.

Guests usually bring gifts. Appropriate house gifts include fruit, pastries, cookies, and sweets. People rarely bring flowers, although, in formal situations, it is traditional after greeting someone to place a garland around his or her neck. A more lavish gift for a Muslim might be a silver compass, so he or she may find the direction of Mecca at prayer time.

This woman *(left)* places her hands together in the Indian greeting position, which is represented by the word *namaste*. While westerners say hello and shake hands, namaste loosely translates to "I honor the place within you in which the entire Universe dwells." Children *(above)* are playing cricket in the streets of Mumbai (Bombay). Cricket is a field sport that was first introduced by the British when they were a colonial power in India. India and Pakistan have some of the best professional cricket players in the world.

Here we see a tray of materials to be used for Rakshabandhan, the Hindu festival of brotherly love. The sisters in the family tie specially made thread bracelets, called *rakhis*, around their brothers' wrists to protect them from evil. This custom illustrates the importance of family ties in Hinduism.

When a man gives a gift to a woman, he explains that it is also from his wife, sister, or mother. Otherwise, it would be too personal.

Hindu Caste and Dharma

A society is a group of people who agree on how to behave. For Hindus, Jains, Sikhs, and Buddhists, this "duty" is called *dharma*. For centuries, the Hindu caste social system shaped most of Indian society. Hindus accepted this system because they believed a person's caste matched their inborn nature, or *guna*. Today, the demands of caste are still primary considerations for many Hindus.

Traditionally, guna determines caste and therefore dharma. Life's tasks and achievements lie along set paths. People walk these paths as individuals. Not everyone is equally successful or devout. Still, there are rules. There is no mobility among castes. If Brahmins "lose" caste by committing murder, lower castes will not accept them.

Ancient caste distinctions were based on spiritual "cleanliness." Brahmin priests were considered the most clean and closest to heaven. Money could not elevate a member of an "unclean" caste to higher social status. "Polluted" castes had no hope of social change in this life.

In 528 BC, the Buddha rejected the idea of caste. Buddhism continued to flourish for the next thousand years. Then, the idea of caste reasserted itself. In the eighteenth century, it weakened for the second time. Early in the twentieth century, Gandhi denounced the idea of "untouchability." (People having no caste were often referred to as "untouchables.") He led a nationwide campaign to end discrimination against untouchables and other lower castes. After independence, the Indian constitution outlawed untouchability. It tried to fix the problem through affirmative action. It reserved places in public institutions for people who had been untouchables.

Today, the caste system persists for a majority of Hindus. Caste loyalty is immense. Members of the smaller upper castes often cannot gain enough votes from members of the larger lower castes to win political seats. Lower-caste members vote for

These two men *(right)* are members of different castes. The priest *(top)* is a member of a high caste, while the fisherman *(bottom)* is a member of a lower caste. There are an estimated 40,000 different castes within India.

each other or run themselves. People tend to support the social and political ideas of members of their own castes.

Muslims and the "Scheduled Tribes"

Only Hindus observe the caste system, a social position one inherits by birth, while Buddhists believe that a person is a priest or outcast by his or her behavior. Muslim society in India was based on class. In a class society, people can be "high" born or "low" born. Descendants of aristocratic families are considered superior to common people. However, Muslims have never believed one person could be born more spiritually pure than another. Prayer, charity, fasting, and the *hajj* are the same for all Muslims. A devout commoner is holier in the eyes of God than a sinful aristocrat. However, while theoretically only Hindus observe the caste system, caste continues to be a defining feature for many Muslims in India.

The other large Indian population that does not use the caste system is tribal. There are more than 500 tribes in India. Fifty-two million people belong to them, roughly 5 percent of the population. Tribe members are religious "animists." Animists worship natural forces rather than the gods or god of Hinduism, Buddhism, and Islam.

Most Indian tribes live in non-urban, non-agricultural settings like forests. They hunt and forage for food rather than farm or trade. Their societies resemble large, extended families. Contact with the modern world has changed the lifestyles of many of these dwindling tribes.

Tribes that have had less contact with the outside world have changed less. The Pakhtuns of northwest Pakistan still govern themselves through *jirgas*, or councils of elders. They have blended their tribal customs with the *sharia* (laws) of Islam.

Other tribes have adapted to modern life. The Todas of the Nilgiri Hills, for example, still live in their native region, but they also raise dairy buffalo and practice trading.

Indian Games

A major feature of Indian daily life is entertainment. India has produced some of the world's best games. The most famous is chess, or *chataranga*, named for the four parts of an Indian army: the chariot, the elephant, the horse, and the foot soldier. The pieces from early chess sets are tiny carvings of these figures. Chess developed in the sixth century and immediately spread north to China and west to Persia, Arabia, and Europe.

The next most popular board game is backgammon, or *chaupar*. Originally Persian, chaupar is an Indian favorite. Indians also gamble with cards and dice.

In the countryside, people enjoy animal games, like horse, camel, and elephant racing. There are fairs at most festivals and farming holidays to demonstrate people's fastest animals. Cockfighting and bearbaiting are common. Pigeon owners set their pigeons aloft to hijack and return with the birds of their opponents.

One oddly aggressive Indian game is kite flying. People coat the strings of their diamond-shaped paper kites with glue and powdered glass. If two kites cross, the glass-coated string of one will sever the

These children are playing a board game in the streets of Mumbai.

Elephant polo is an ancient sport in India. It is played with two teams of three elephants each. A polo player and a *mahout* both ride the elephant, the mahout guiding the animal while the player tries to knock the polo ball in the goal.

string of the other. When the severed kite leaps free, people chase after it.

Children chase adult kites, or fly their own. They also play with tops, yo-yos, and hobbyhorses. A child's game of skill is to drive a waist-high metal hoop along a road with a piece of wire.

Indian Sports

Centuries of Indian court painting reveal that the upper classes have always enjoyed hunting, archery, and falconry. Indians are also fond of polo, which was introduced by the Muslims in the thirteenth century. Polo is sometimes called *chaugan*, which is the Persian word for a stick or mallet.

Polo is a grueling sport. It was designed to train cavalry officers to think and move as a team while on horseback. The Mughal nobility adored it and turned it into a pleasure sport. When the British arrived, they also loved it. They built polo clubs in India and at home and spread the sport to both North and South America. In the West, Polo is usually associated with the rich, though in India, it is also popular among the people of the Indus River Valley, a region known for fast, scrappy ponies.

The Indians took to Western sports with a passion. Cricket and hockey are both national pastimes. The Calcutta Cricket Club dates to 1792. The first all-Indian cricket club, the Orient Cricket Club in Bombay (Mumbai), was founded in 1848. By 1912, there was a regular cricket quadrangle of Hindu, Parsi, British, and Muslim teams.

In the twentieth century, women took up badminton, tennis, and table tennis. Girls' schools offered hockey, volleyball, and cricket. Women's cricket is now a major sport.

EDUCATION AND WORK IN INDIA

I ndia's educational tradition is ancient. In Hindu villages, primary schools, or *pathshalas*, have long taught reading, writing, and arithmetic. This elementary level historically welcomed members of different castes, as well as girls. A similar type of school, a *maktab*, operated in Muslim villages.

At higher levels, education was linked more closely to religion. Older Brahmin students attended Hindu *tols*. They studied sacred texts, mathematics, astronomy, logic, and law. Classes were taught in Sanskrit. At Muslim *madrasas*, similar subjects were taught in Persian or Arabic.

Focused on the search for enlightenment, Buddhist monasteries welcomed all seekers of knowledge. They attracted powerful rulers and rich merchants. Money from these patrons enabled the Buddhists to build such intellectual and spiritual retreats as Nalanda and Vikramshila at Bihar, and Takshashila in Pakistan. At one time, the red brick walls of Nalanda housed 10,000 students and 2,000 teachers. Its campus of monasteries, temples, and dense green lawns covered thirty-five acres (fourteen hectares).

Education flourished during the Mughal Empire until the empire collapsed in the eighteenth century. Established schools were abandoned, partly due to India's British occupation, the British having little interest in the Indian school system. The British were in India exclusively for trade and profit, and their interests were in its businesses and

Educational experiences are diverse in India. This teacher *(left)* instructs students at the Angels Montessori school in Mananbur, Kerala. Montessori's philosophy of education is that children learn best when they are in a social environment that supports each individual's unique development. In 1911, the Order of World Scouts was founded by Sir Francis Vane in London, and it spawned the group we know today as the Boy Scouts. As part of the former British Empire, Indian nationals adopted the scouting tradition, as shown by these boys *(above)* in Gujarat.

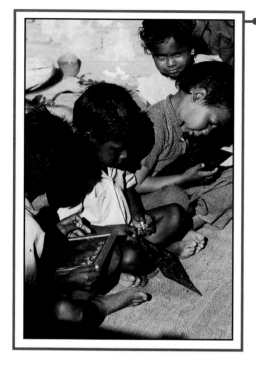

Recently, a constitutional amendment in India made education for children ages six to fourteen years a fundamental right, but the quality of education for Indian children continues to vary. These children are studying with chalk and slate in the slums of Jaipur.

its army. In time, British businesses expanded and needed more staff. Their solution was to train Indians for English-speaking jobs.

By 1835, the British set aside government funds for an Indian educational system. The system was secular (non-religious) and taught European literature and Western science. It drained money from existing Indian schools. Buddhist and Muslim groups fought this trend. They believed religion and education were deeply linked. In the end, they failed. The British raj created India's first standardized school system.

The British system was not nationwide and most government money went to city schools. These developed a class of Western-educated Indians—mainly upper-caste men—to work in British offices. As a result, less money and fewer resources went to rural areas, members of low castes, and women.

Indians objected to this discrimination. In 1910, nationalist leader G. K. Gokhale fought to make education free and attainable for every child in the country. Eleven years later, in 1921, a version of the law passed. Education became widely available and required in most regions.

Schools in Modern India

Today, primary education is free in government schools for children between

Western-style education is available to wealthier children in the cities. These suited-up boys are being escorted to the New Era School, where they will gain valuable English language skills.

Old beliefs deem education to be a waste of time for a girl who will marry at thirteen years of age and be occupied serving her husband and his family, but these girls defy this myth. Women are making steady progress in the world of education and work in India.

the ages of six and fourteen in all of the Indian states. Since independence, the number of schools has mushroomed. Most are coeducational. There are differences between urban and rural areas, and in some rural states such as Nagaland and Himachal Pradesh the number of children attending classes is lower. Despite improvements, fifty million Indian children remain outside the educational system. More than two-thirds of these are girls.

In 1995, a Hyderabad organization called the MV Foundation created a yearlong residential school for girls between the ages of nine and fourteen. It continues to provide an intensive education and encourages curiosity and questions. This is a new experience for many Indian girls, most of whom cannot read. A typical student might have spent her childhood working twelve-hour days in a small factory or in a field picking flowers for the equivalent of twenty-eight cents an hour.

The biggest obstacle to the program is not money, but parental approval. For many parents, it makes little sense to educate girls who will marry at thirteen and then devote themselves to their husbands' families. For girls who do attend, the next step is entrance exams to secondary school where they will begin grade seven.

Secondary school is usually standard only for college-bound students. Young

The title of this book is *A Day in the Life of a Typical Rural Girl*, and it probably doesn't involve school. Only a third of girls in India have a primary school education, and it is most difficult for girls in rural communities who may have heavy work responsibilities, even at a young age.

Although India has reduced its poverty rate from a staggering 55 percent in the 1970s to 35 percent today, an estimated 350 million Indians continue to live below the poverty line, and two-thirds of Indian children are malnourished.

people who plan on technical or craft professions apprentice themselves at an early age or go straight to work. Half of India's secondary schools are private and costly to attend. The rest lack funds and equipment. Children of wealthy families normally attend private school and are better educated and more likely to go to college. With college degrees, these students will eventually get better paying jobs and send their own children to college. This continuous cycle maintains the gap between India's intellectual elite and its less-educated masses.

India's university system is the oldest and most sophisticated in South Asia. After those of the United States and Russia, it is the third largest in the world. Its first modern college, Presidency College, was founded in Calcutta in 1817. In 1857, the British used London University as a model for the Universities of Calcutta, Bombay (Mumbai), and Madras (Chennai).

Since independence, colleges and universities have developed all over the country, most based on British models.

Work and Unemployment

A modern educational system prepares students to work. Unfortunately, Indian unemployment is about 20 percent of its population. Nearly 35 percent of Indians live below the poverty line. In traditional Indian society, people who could not support themselves depended on their families or the community for care. In recent years, however, many communities have changed. A village is no longer an extended family and people have less contact with their neighbors. In cities today, as in many cities around the world, people may not know their neighbors at all.

To help this problem, India has created work programs. These provide a guaranteed number of work hours to at least one person in a poverty-stricken family. Many of India's 600,000 villages have barely adequate water supplies and no electricity. One government program, the Integrated Rural Development

Program (IRDP), targets poor rural families. The IRDP teaches agricultural skills and provides pumps, wells, and fertilizer to Indian farms. In the early 1980s, the program helped three million Indian families.

The Indian Economy

India is rich in natural resources and has an enormous work force, yet it is classified as a developing country. This is partly because India has not yet reached its full potential. During the raj, the British used India as a source of raw materials for the West. This destroyed much of India's industry.

These men are working in the world's largest open cast coal mine in Dhambad, Bihar. Commercial exploitation of minerals and other natural resources have not only endangered forests but have jeopardized the survival of local nomadic tribes whose lifestyle is based on hunting and fishing.

Since independence, the country has grown rapidly. India's first great technological achievement after independence was self-reliance in food production. This was called the Green Revolution. (Later, there was also a White Revolution, for dairy products.) It took the cooperation of farmers, bioscientists, and government agencies. Scientists developed new seed types, expanded irrigation, and introduced pesticides and chemical fertilizers.

Technology is bridging a gap between India's ancient and venerable past and its progressive future. Here we see the Dalai Lama, the Tibetan spiritual leader-in-exile, curiously viewing the Web site of Kiran Bedi, India's first female police officer.

Indian space research dates to 1961, when the country established the Indian National Committee for Space Research (INCOSPAR). The first Indian satellite, *Aryabhatta*, was launched in 1975. In 1974, India became the world's sixth nuclear power.

Modern India has made dramatic progress in telecommunications and information technology. Satellites link India's tiny villages with telephones, radios, and television networks. India designed its own supercomputers (the Param series) without foreign aid. Software export rises annually and is the product of the most skilled software engineers in the world. Prime Minister Vajpayee recently remarked, "I believe IT [information technology] is India's tomorrow."

The Future of India

India's landscape is never quiet. The country struggles with illiteracy, rural poverty, and social discrimination. There are droughts, flash floods, severe thunderstorms, and earthquakes. The environment suffers from deforestation, soil erosion, over-grazing, pollution, and a staggering population. In July 2002, the total population of India was 1,045,845,226.

Sikh separatists agitate in Punjab. The relationship with Pakistan smolders. Tensions between Hindus and Muslims flare periodically into violence. In 2002, Gujurat witnessed some of the worst rioting between Hindu and Muslim mobs that India had seen in a decade.

On the other hand, for fifty years of independence, India has fed its immense population mostly without international aid. It has modernized its industry and agriculture. Cutting-edge technology and manufacturing have made it a major industrial power. One of the signs of a great democracy is a free press. The Indian press is free, intelligent, and highly critical of government failings.

India is both an ancient country and a young republic. Its struggles ahead loom large. In the years to come, the Indian government must look inward to improve the lives and opportunities of its people. At the same time, the country will have to focus beyond its borders, on its place among the nations of the world. Given the length and breadth of its history, India is certain to play a large part in the global future.

INDIA
AT A GLANCE

HISTORY

India's Indus Valley civilization dates back more than 4,000 years. It is one of the oldest in the world. In 1500 BC, Aryan nomads invaded from the northwest and conquered the Indus River Valley. They imposed their Vedic religion on the native people. Over time, Vedism absorbed some of the ideas of native Indian religions and evolved into Hinduism.

In the fourth century BC, the Nanda dynasty took control of much of India. The Mauryas succeeded them. The Mauryan emperor Asoka was India's first Buddhist ruler. The Mauryas fell to a group of Brahmins, who were followed by the Bactrian Greeks, the Scythians, the Parthians, and then, in the first century AD, the central Asian Kushanas. The Indian Guptas wiped out the Kushanas and began the Indian Classical Age.

In the seventh century, the Rajputs of Rajasthan rose to power. Their constant civil wars allowed Muslim invaders to conquer northern India. The

Jawaharlal Nehru

Muslims slowly expanded their empire to the south. A series of Muslim regimes culminated in the Mughal Empire. The Mughal emperor Akbar unified much of the region. His grandson Shah Jahan fostered the arts and built Delhi's Red Fort and Taj Mahal. Under the Mughals, northern India developed a sophisticated culture that combined native and Persian elements.

In the fifteenth century, Portuguese traders arrived from Europe. Over the next 300 years, the Mughals became dependent on European trade. By the late eighteenth century, the British East India Company controlled much of India. In 1765, the Mughals granted the company financial control of the lands around Calcutta in Bengal. In 1857, a group of Indian soldiers, or sepoys, rose against the British. When the British regained control, Queen Victoria disbanded the British East India Company and crowned herself sovereign empress of India.

Under the British rule, or raj, Indians were second-class citizens in their own country. Indian dissatisfaction grew. Mohandas Gandhi and Jawaharlal Nehru spearheaded a "Quit India" campaign to drive the British out of the country. Their tactics of nonviolent resistance won India's independence in 1947.

At the time of independence, Hindu-Muslim differences led to the partition of the country into secular India and Muslim Pakistan. The northeast and north-west corners of India became East and West Pakistan. In 1971, a war between India and Pakistan ended with East Pakistan becoming the independent nation of Bangladesh.

Today, India and Pakistan have an ongoing dispute over the northern territory of Jammu and Kashmir. Hindu-Muslim tensions still erupt periodically into violence. Other national problems include overpopulation, poverty, and environmental issues. At the same time, India is a leader in high technology and has made impressive economic gains in its five decades as a free democracy.

ECONOMY

India's economy is based on traditional village farming, modern agriculture, industry, support services, and handicrafts. Machines still cannot match the refinement of traditional Indian handicrafts. Woven products provide employment and income for a significant portion of India's rural population. Traditional textiles are equally popular in India and abroad, and major exports include hand-knotted carpets, art metal ware, hand-printed textiles, brocaded silks, and leather, wood, and cane wares.

Indian industry produces textiles, chemicals, processed food, steel, transportation equipment, cement, mining products, petroleum, machinery, and software. The most important of these products for export are textiles, gemstones and jewelry, engineering goods, chemicals, and leather goods.

Indian livestock farmers raise cattle, water buffalo, sheep, goats, and poultry. Along India's roughly 4,375 miles (7,000 km) of coastline, the fishing industry is a large part of its economy. Village farms and plantations produce rice, wheat, oilseed, cotton, jute, tea, sugarcane, and potatoes.

India is the world's largest producer of legal opium for the global pharmaceutical market. An unknown amount of this opium is also sold on the black market of the international drug trade. Additionally, India produces such illegal substances as hashish and methaqualone and is a transit point for illicit narcotics produced in neighboring nations.

India imports machinery, fertilizer, chemicals, and crude oil. Fossil fuels like crude oil are responsible for nearly 80 percent of Indian electrical power. The rest comes mainly from hydropower (18 percent) and nuclear power (3 percent).

As of October 2000, there were 30 million telephone lines and 3 million mobile phones in India's major cities. This puts telephone density at about 2 phones per 100 people. Currently, there is a telephone waiting list of more than two million. In some rural areas, the phone system still uses now-obsolete manual switchboards.

The domestic satellite system includes 254 earth stations. This supports 43 Internet service providers and 4.5 million Internet users. Broadcasts reach 116 million radios and, in a country of a billion people, only 63 million televisions.

As India entered the twenty-first century, its gross domestic product was growing at a rate of 6 percent. This economic health is due in large part to booming exports of software services. At the same time, more than a third of the population cannot afford adequate food. In addition, electricity shortages continue in many regions.

There is a dramatic class division in India between the rich and the poor. The top 10 percent of India's population consumes one-third of domestic and imported goods and services. The lowest 10 percent of the population consumes 3 percent.

GOVERNMENT AND POLITICS

India is a federal republic. It won its independence from the United Kingdom on August 15, 1947. Its constitution dates to January 26, 1950. India has both a president, who is the chief of state, and a prime minister, who is the head of government.

From the age of eighteen, all Indian citizens have the right to vote. In the presidential election, they vote for an electoral college. This college is made up of members of parliament and members of the state legislatures. Electoral members elect a president into office for a five-year term. The people do not vote for the prime minister; this is the responsibility of parliamentary members of the majority party.

Currently, India's president is A. P. J. Abdul Kalam. The vice president is Bhairon Singh Shekhawat. The prime minister is Atal Bihari Vajpayee. Vajpayee served in the parliament for four decades and was first elected prime minister in 1996. In addition to the three heads of state, the Indian government has a Council of Ministers. The president appoints these ministers at the recommendation of the prime minister.

Following the English model, the Indian parliament, or Sansad, is made up of a Council of States, or Rajya Sabha, and a People's Assembly, or Lok Sabha. There are not more than 250 members in the Rajya Sabha. The president appoints twelve of these. Elected members of the state and territorial assemblies choose the rest. Members serve six-year terms. The Lok Sabha has 545 seats. The president appoints only two Lok Sabha seats. A popular election selects the other 543. Members serve five-year terms.

The Indian legal system is based on English common law. It allows limited judicial review of legislative acts. The Supreme Court is made up of judges appointed by the president. These judges remain in office until the age of sixty-five.

India is made up of twenty-eight states and seven union territories. Major political parties include the Bharatiya Janata Party (BJP), the All India Anna Dravida Munnetra Kazhagam (AIADMK), the All India Forward Bloc (AIFB), the Communist Party of India (CPI), the Communist Party of India/Marxist-Leninist (CPI/ML), Congress (I) Party, the Indian National League, the Muslim League, the Nationalist Congress Party (NCP), the National Democratic Alliance, and the Revolutionary Socialist Party (RSP).

Numerous groups pressure the government for changes in legal and land rulings that affect their interests. The government also fields the demands of separatists. Separatists want greater regional independence.

India has ongoing disputes with Pakistan over the status of Jammu and Kashmir and Indus River water rights. Its borders with China and Bangladesh are also a constant source of disagreement. Bangladesh also contests India's rights to New Moore/South Talpatty Island.

TIMELINE

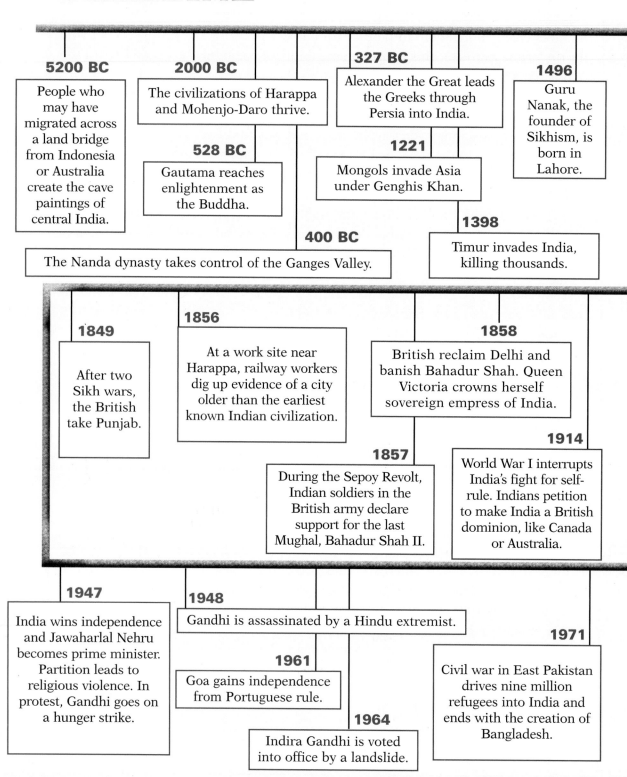

5200 BC
People who may have migrated across a land bridge from Indonesia or Australia create the cave paintings of central India.

2000 BC
The civilizations of Harappa and Mohenjo-Daro thrive.

327 BC
Alexander the Great leads the Greeks through Persia into India.

1496
Guru Nanak, the founder of Sikhism, is born in Lahore.

528 BC
Gautama reaches enlightenment as the Buddha.

1221
Mongols invade Asia under Genghis Khan.

400 BC
The Nanda dynasty takes control of the Ganges Valley.

1398
Timur invades India, killing thousands.

1849
After two Sikh wars, the British take Punjab.

1856
At a work site near Harappa, railway workers dig up evidence of a city older than the earliest known Indian civilization.

1858
British reclaim Delhi and banish Bahadur Shah. Queen Victoria crowns herself sovereign empress of India.

1857
During the Sepoy Revolt, Indian soldiers in the British army declare support for the last Mughal, Bahadur Shah II.

1914
World War I interrupts India's fight for self-rule. Indians petition to make India a British dominion, like Canada or Australia.

1947
India wins independence and Jawaharlal Nehru becomes prime minister. Partition leads to religious violence. In protest, Gandhi goes on a hunger strike.

1948
Gandhi is assassinated by a Hindu extremist.

1961
Goa gains independence from Portuguese rule.

1964
Indira Gandhi is voted into office by a landslide.

1971
Civil war in East Pakistan drives nine million refugees into India and ends with the creation of Bangladesh.

1510

The Portuguese capture island of Goa.

1526

India is invaded by Babur, establishing the rule of the Mughals.

1556

Akbar is proclaimed the successor of Humayun.

1600

Queen Elizabeth I gives the British East India Company trading rights.

1658

Aurangzeb becomes the Mughal emperor. His enforcement of Islamic law conflicts with Hindu powers.

1816–1818

The British subdue the northwestern Marathas.

1765

The Mughal emperor grants the East India Company the right to Bengali revenues. British power in India grows.

1915

Mohandas Gandhi works to make the INC an all-India party, which includes the poor, illiterate, those of "unclean" caste, and women.

1919

General Reginald Dyer orders his troops to fire on a peaceful protest in Amritsar, killing 379 people.

1922

An archaeological team excavates Mohenjo-Daro.

1920s–1947

Tension increases between the INC and the Muslim League, who want a separate Muslim state.

1984

The bid to turn Punjab into a Sikh nation ends when Indira Gandhi orders a siege on a Sikh temple, which kills 600 people. Soon after, she is assassinated.

1996

India's current prime minister, Shri Atal Bihari Vajpayee, is voted into office.

2000

Overall death tolls in Jammu and Kashmir related to control of the region climb to 21,000 people.

2001

A. P. J. Abdul Kalam is elected president.

2002

Tensions in Jammu and Kashmir intensify. India and Pakistan both threaten to declare war.

INDIA

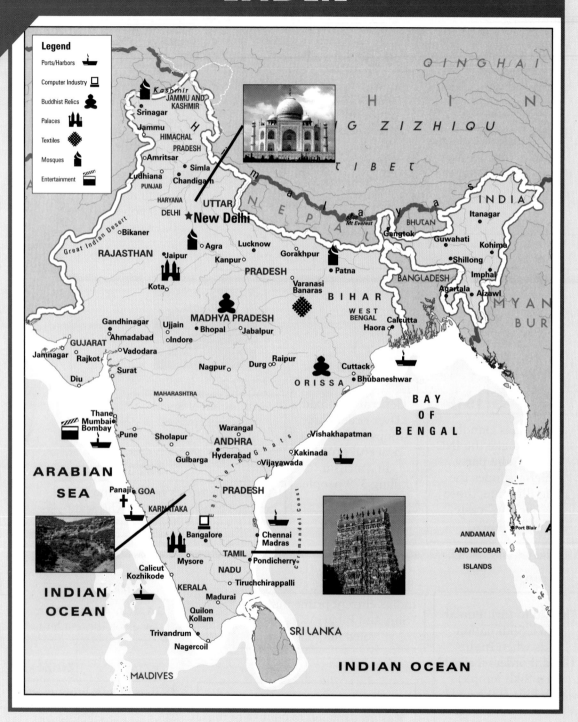

Legend
- Ports/Harbors
- Computer Industry
- Buddhist Relics
- Palaces
- Textiles
- Mosques
- Entertainment

QINGHAI

ZIZHIQU

TIBET

Kashmir
JAMMU AND KASHMIR
• Srinagar
• Jammu
HIMACHAL PRADESH
• Amritsar
• Simla
Ludhiana
PUNJAB
• Chandigarh
HARYANA
DELHI
★ **New Delhi**

INDIA
• Itanagar
BHUTAN
• Gangtok
• Guwahati
• Kohima
• Shillong
• Imphal
• Agartala • Aizawl
BANGLADESH
MYAN
BUR

• Bikaner
RAJASTHAN
• Jaipur
• Agra
• Lucknow
• Kanpur
• Gorakhpur
PRADESH
• Patna
Kota
Varanasi Banaras
BIHAR
WEST BENGAL
• Calcutta
• Haora

Great Indian Desert

• Gandhinagar
• Ahmadabad
• Ujjain
MADHYA PRADESH
• Bhopal
• Jabalpur
GUJARAT
• Vadodara
• Indore
Jamnagar
• Rajkot
• Surat
Diu

• Nagpur
• Durg
• Raipur
ORISSA
• Cuttack
• Bhubaneshwar

MAHARASHTRA

BAY OF BENGAL

Thane
Mumbai
Bombay
• Pune
• Sholapur
• Warangal
ANDHRA
• Gulbarga
Hyderabad
• Vijayawada
• Kakinada
• Vishakhapatman

ARABIAN SEA

Panaji GOA
KARNATAKA
• Bangalore
PRADESH
Coromandel Coast
Eastern Ghats

INDIAN OCEAN

• Mysore
• Chennai Madras
TAMIL
• Pondicherry
NADU
• Calicut Kozhikode
KERALA
• Madurai
• Tiruchchirappalli
• Quilon Kollam
• Trivandrum
• Nagercoil

ANDAMAN AND NICOBAR ISLANDS
• Port Blair

SRI LANKA

MALDIVES

INDIAN OCEAN

Mt Everest
NEPAL
Himalayas

ECONOMIC FACT SHEET

GDP in US$: $2.2 trillion

GDP Sectors: Agriculture 25%, industry 24%, services 51%

Land Use: Arable land 56%, permanent crops 1%, permanent pastures 4%, forests and woodland 23%, other 16%

Currency: Indian rupee (INR): 46.540 rupees to the US dollar

Workforce: Agriculture 67%, services 18%, industry 15%

Major Agricultural Products: Rice, wheat, oilseed, cotton, jute, tea, sugarcane, potatoes, cattle, water buffalo, sheep, goats, poultry

Major Exports: $43.1 billion—textiles, gems, jewelry, engineering products, chemicals, leather products

Major Imports: $60.8 billion—crude oil, machinery, gems, fertilizer, chemicals

Significant Trading Partners:

   Imports: Benelux (Belgium, the Netherlands and Luxembourg), Germany, Japan, Saudi Arabia, United Kingdom, United States

   Exports: Germany, Hong Kong, Japan, United Arab Emirates, United Kingdom, United States

Rate of Unemployment: Approximately 20%

Highways: Total 2,074,778 miles (3,319,644 km)

Railroads: Total 39,808 miles (63,693 km)

Waterways: Total 10,113 miles (16,180 km), navigable by large vessels 2,269 miles (3,631 km)

Airports: Total 337 (paved 235, unpaved 102), heliports 16

POLITICAL FACT SHEET

Official Country Name:
Republic of India

Capital: New Delhi

System of Government:
Federal Republic

Federal Structure: President, vice president, prime minister, parliament made up of a Council of States and a People's Assembly

Government Structure: India's bicameral parliament is composed of the Rajya Sabha and the Lok Sabha. The Rajya Sabha currently consists of 245 members. The Lok Sabha currently consists of 543 members.

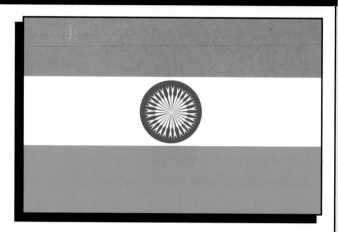

National Anthem: *Jana Gana Mana Adhinayaka* by Rabindranath Tagore, adopted by the Constituent Assembly, January 24, 1950

> *Thou art the rulers of the minds of all people, Dispenser of India's destiny.*
> *Thy name rouses the hearts of Punjab, Sind, Gujarat, and Maratha,*
> *Of the Dravida, and Orissa, and Bengal;*
> *It echoes in the hills of the Vindhyasand Himalayas,*
> *Mingles in the music of Yamuna and Ganga*
> *And is chanted by the waves of the Indian Sea.*
> *They pray for thy blessings and sing thy praise.*
> *The saving of all people waits in thy hand, thou dispenser of India's destiny,*
> *Victory, victory, victory to thee.*

Administrative Divisions (Twenty-eight states and seven union territories): Andaman and Nicobar Islands, Andhra Pradesh, Arunachal Pradesh, Assam, Bihar, Chandigarh, Chhattisgarh, Dadra and Nagar Haveli, Daman and Diu, Delhi, Goa, Gujarat, Haryana, Himachal Pradesh, Jammu and Kashmir, Jharkhand, Karnataka, Kerala, Lakshadweep, Madhya Pradesh, Maharashtra, Manipur, Meghalaya, Mizoram, Nagaland, Orissa, Pondicherry, Punjab, Rajasthan, Sikkim, Tamil Nadu, Tripura, Uttaranchal, Uttar Pradesh, West Bengal

Independence: August 15, 1947 (from UK)

Constitution: January 26, 1950

Legal System: Based on English common law; limited judicial review of legislative acts

Suffrage: Eighteen years of age; universal

Number of Registered Voters: 984,003,683 voters out of a population of 1,045,845,226

CULTURAL FACT SHEET

Official Languages: Hindi, Bengali, Telugu, Marathi, Tamil, Urdu, Gujurati, Malayalam, Kannada, Oriya, Punjabi, Assamese, Kashmiri, Sindhi, Sanskrit, and English

Major Religions: Hindu 78.3%, Muslim 15%, Christian 2.3%, Sikh 1.9%, other 2.5%

Ethnic Groups: Indo-Aryan 72%, Dravidian 25%, Mongoloid and other 3%

Life Expectancy: Total 62.86 years

Time: New Delhi time is Greenwich Mean Time + 5:30 hours

Literacy Rate: 52% (male 65.5%, female 37.7%)

National Flower: Lotus or water lily

National Bird: Peacock

National Animal: Tiger

National Tree: Banyan

Cultural Leaders:

Visual Arts: Amrita Shergill, M. F. Husain, Krishen Khanna, Anjan Banerjee, Ashim Ghosh, Kaustav Biswas, Sheila Kapoor, Suvra Chatterjee

Literature: Rabindranath Tagore, Anita Desai, Ruth Prawer Jhabvala, Vikram Seth, R. K. Narayan, Zulfikar Ghose, Salman Rushdie

Entertainment: Amitabh Bacchan, Aamir Khan, Akshay Kumar, Anil Kapoor, Aishwarya Rai, Karisma Kapoor, Raveena Tandon, Sridevi, Ranadhir Roy, V. J. Jog, Sruti Sadolikar, Ali Akbar Khan

Sports: Vangipurappu Laxman (cricket), Anju Jain (cricket), Nirupama Vaidyanathan (tennis), Mahesh Bhupathi (tennis)

National Holidays and Festivals

As most Indian holidays fall according to religious or non-standard calendars, the dates vary from year to year. The following list is in chronological order from January to December with firm dates included where applicable.

Pongal—Harvest festival

Republic Day—January 26; national constitution

Id-ul-Azha—Islamic commemoration of the sacrifice of Abraham

Muhurram—Shi'ite Muslims commemorate the martyrdom of Imam Hussain, grandson of the prophet Muhammad

Holi—Spring festival

Mahavir Jayanti—Birth of Vardhamana Mahavira

Baisakhi—Hindu solar new year

Buddha Purnima—Enlightenment of Buddha

Khardad Sal—Birth of the prophet Zarathustra

Janmashtami—Birth of Krishna

Independence Day—August 15; anniversary of Indian independence

Onam—Kerala's harvest festival

Dussehra and Durga Puja—Celebration of the triumph of Rama over Ravana

Gandhi Jayanti—October 2: birthday of Mohandas Gandhi

Diwali—Festival of lights

Guru Nanak Jayanti—Birthday of Guru Nanak, founder of Sikism

Children's Day—November 14; birthday of Nehru and a celebration of children

Id-ul-Fitr—End of Muslim fasting month

GLOSSARY

Aryans (AIR-ee-ins) A nomadic people of Eurasian descent who invaded India in 1500 BC.

Brahmin (BRAH-men) A member of the highest, priestly Hindu caste, which is based on ideas dating back to the Aryan invaders of 1500 BC.

Brahminism (BRAH-meh-nih-zum) An evolutionary stage of the Hindu religion that occurred after Aryan Vedism but before the Hinduism of classical India.

Buddhism (BOO-dih-zum) A religion based on the idea of detachment from the desire that is the root of all suffering. It was developed by Siddhartha Gautama, who reached enlightenment and became known as the Buddha.

caste (KAST) Level in a social hierarchy developed by the Aryan invaders and continuing to the present day; the levels divide into Brahmins (priests), Kshatriyas (rulers), Vaishyas (merchants), and Shudras (laborers); prior to modern reforms, there were also people regarded as "untouchables," who were considered to be beneath the caste system.

dharma (DAR-muh) One's duty in light of one's place in society and the universe.

dhoti (DO-tee) A man's loincloth.

Hinduism (HIN-doo-ih-zum) A religion that developed out of the ancient Vedic beliefs of the Aryans and has since absorbed ideas of Buddhism and Jainism.

incarnation (in-car-NAY-shun) A bodily manifestation of a supernatural being, like Vishnu's appearances on Earth, or a period of time spent in a given body, like the different human lifetimes of reincarnation.

Islam (IS-lom) The monotheistic religion of Muslims, who worship Allah and follow the teachings of the prophet Muhammad.

Jainism (Jeye-nih-zum) A religion based on the idea of *ahimsa*, or nonviolence.

karma (KAR-muh) One's fate based on the actions and occurrences of one's previous life.

Maharajah (mah-hah-RAH-jah) A Hindu ruler of a princely state.

Mamluks (MAM-luks) Turkish and Caucasian slaves imported by Islamic rulers to form loyal armies.

Muslim (MUZ-lum) A follower of Islam.

Nawab (nah-WAB) A Muslim ruler of a princely state.

raj (RAHJ) The Hindi word for "rule," used to describe a political regime like the British raj.

raja (RAH-jaa) A king.

rani (RAH-nee) A queen.

reincarnation (ree-in-kar-NAY-shun) Rebirth of the soul in another body.

sari (SAR-ee) A dress worn by Indian women created by wrapping a long, seamless piece of silk or cotton around the waist and tossing the end over one shoulder.

secular (SEK-kyuh-lur) Not religious.

Sikhism (SEE-kih-zum) A new religion developed by Guru Nanak to answer divisive issues between the religions of Hinduism and Islam.

Vedas (VAY-duhs) The sacred writings of the Aryans, the first of which, the Rig Veda, dates to the time of the Aryan invasion in 1500 BC. "Veda" means "knowledge" in Sanskrit.

FOR MORE INFORMATION

American Institute of Indian Studies
1130 East 59th Street
Chicago, IL 60637
(773) 702 8638
Web site: http://www.indiastudies.org

Asia Society and Museum
725 Park Avenue
New York, NY 10021
(212) 288-6400
Web site: http://www.asiasociety.org

Canadian Asian Studies
  Association (CASA)
University of Montreal
CP 6128, Succ.
Centre-ville
Montreal, PQ H3C 3J7
Canada
Web site: http://www.casa.umontreal.ca/htm/
  maine.htm

Embassy of India
2107 Massachusetts Avenue
Washington, DC 20008
(202) 939-7000
Web site: http://www.indianembassy.org

National Museum of India, New Delhi
Janpath, New Delhi 110011
India
Web site: http://www.
  nationalmuseumindia.org

Web Sites

Due to the changing nature of Internet links, the Rosen Publishing Group, Inc., has developed an online list of Web sites related to the subject of this book. This site is updated regularly. Please use this link to access the list:

http://www.rosenlinks.com/pswc/indi/

FOR FURTHER READING

Dommermuth-Costa, Carol. *Indira Gandhi: Daughter of India*. Minneapolis: Lerner Publications Company: 2001.

Frere, Mary. *Old Deccan Days or Hindoo Fairy Legends*. New York: Dover, 1967.

Kalman, Bobbie. *India: The Culture*. New York: Crabtree Publishing, 2000.

Kipling, Rudyard. *Kim*. New York: Viking, 1992.

Krishnaswami, Uma. *Shower of Gold: Girls and Women in the Stories of India*. North Haven, CT: Linnet Books, 1999.

Menen, Aubrey. *The Ramayana*. New York: Charles Scribner's Sons, 1954.

Ness, Caroline. *The Ocean of Story: Fairy Tales from India*. New York: Lothrop Lee & Shepard, 1996.

Staples, Suzanne Fisher. *Shiva's Fire*. New York: Farrar, Straus & Giroux, 2000.

BIBLIOGRAPHY

Archer, W. G. *The Loves of Krishna in Indian Painting and Poetry*. New York: Macmillan, 1957.

Buck, William. *Ramayana: King Rama's Way*. New York: New American Library, 1978.

Carrière, Jean-Claude. Peter Brook, trans. *The Mahabharata: A Play Based Upon the Indian Classic Epic*. New York: Harper & Row, 1987.

Craven, Roy C. *Indian Art*. London: Thames & Hudson, 1976.

Ellis, Kirsten. *The Insider's Guide to India*. Hong Kong: CFW Publications, 1990.

Frere, Mary. *Old Deccan Days or Hindoo Fairy Legends*. New York: Dover, 1967.

Goetz, Hermann, *India: Five Thousand Years of Indian Art*. New York: McGraw Hill, 1959.

Hamilton, Elizabeth. *Translations of the Letters of a Hindoo Rajah*. Toronto: Broadview Press, 1999.

Jaffrey, Madhur. *A Taste of India*. New York: Atheneum, 1988.

Keay, John, *India: A History*. New York: Grove Press, 2000.

Menen, Aubrey. *The Ramayana*. New York: Charles Scribner's Sons, 1954.

Moxham, Roy. *The Great Hedge of India*. New York: Carroll & Graf, 2001.

Patnaik, Naveen. *A Second Paradise*. New York: Doubleday, 1985.

Robinson, Francis. *The Cambridge Encyclopedia of India, Pakistan, Bangladesh, Sri Lanka, Nepal, Bhutan, and the Maldives*. New York: Cambridge University Press, 1989.

Sethi, Rajeev. *Aditi: The Living Arts of India*. Washington, DC: Smithsonian Institution Press, 1985.

Tillotson, G. H. R. *Mughal India*. New York: Penguin Books, 1991.

Toh, Irene, and Vivien Crump. *India: Rajasthan*. New York: Alfred A. Knopf, 1996.

Yutang, Lin. *The Wisdom of China and India*. New York: Random House, 1942.

PRIMARY SOURCE IMAGE LIST

Page 18: Ruins of the ancient city of Mohenjo-Daro, part of the Harappan civilization of ancient India. The ruins of Mohenjo-Daro are located in what is now southern Pakistan.

Page 20: This ancient sculpture, thought to be a priest figure from Mohenjo-Daro, is now housed at the Karachi Museum in Pakistan.

Page 21: First- or second-century Gandharan Buddhist sculpture found in Gunbat, India, and now located in the Museo Nazionale d'Arte Orientale in Rome, Italy.

Page 23: This detail is just one of many paintings inside the Buddhist caves at Ajanta, near Maharashtra, India, that date back as early as 200 BC. Once a group of five temples and twenty-four monasteries that were abandoned around AD 650, the caves and the magnificent art they inspired were rediscovered in 1819 by a group of British tiger-hunters.

Page 24: The detailed gateway shown on this page is located at the Sri Meenakshi Sundareswarar Temple in Madurai, India.

Page 27: Miniature painting of the *Akbarnama*, a sixteenth-century Mughal book documenting the reign of Emperor Akbar. This painting is now located in the Victoria and Albert Museum in London, England.

Page 29: Engraving taken from the 1727 book *Voyages* by Jean Albert de Mandelslo that depicts the British trading station of Surat.

Page 30 (top): British political cartoon portraying Earl Charles Canning, governor general of India during the time of the Sepoy Revolt (1857), circa nineteenth century.

Page 30 (bottom): Engraving illustrating the capture of Bahadur Shah II in 1857 by British commander Captain William Hodson, circa 1957. This engraving is located in Delhi, India.

Page 31: Title page for the 1859 book *Campaign in India 1857–1858* by George F. Atkinson that illustrates Indian sepoy soldiers during rifle practice.

Page 32 (top): Photograph of Indian nationalist leader Mohandas Karamchand Gandhi with Indian poet and politician Sarojini Naidu, circa 1930.

Page 32 (bottom): Photograph of mounted British soldiers during a salt raid in progress on the Wadela salt pans in Bombay (Mumbai), India, circa 1930.

Page 33: Congressional resolution passed by Pandit Motilal Nehru that outlines the organizational plan of the independence movement and details India's post-colonial parliamentary-styled government, circa 1947.

Page 35: A political cartoon entitled "India—A Chessboard," circa 1940s, that was among the Indian printed news surrounding the events that led to India's independence from Britain in 1947.

Page 41 (top): Children's book featuring the elephant-headed deity Ganesh illustrated in full-color.

Page 43: Ancient seal from the city of Mohenjo-Daro that features pictographs of an as-of-yet-undeciphered written language, circa 2000 BC. This seal is currently housed in the Karachi Museum in Pakistan.

Page 44: Ancient Brahmi script as seen on a pillar erected during the reign of Asoka (273–232 BC). The pillar itself is located in Sarnath, Varansi, in India.

Page 46: This sixteenth-century watercolor painting of the Ramayana is now located in the Freer Gallery of Art, part of the Smithsonian Institution, in Washington, D.C.

Page 62: Painted detail derived from works inside the Buddhist caves at Ajanta, near Maharashtra, India, that date back as early as 200 BC.

Page 64: Eleventh-century Hindu sculpture found in Madras, India. This piece, known as *Shiva Nataraja*, is now housed at the Victoria and Albert Museum in London, England.

Page 68: Buddhist relics sit beside this bodhi tree in northern India.

Page 74: Located in Hyderabad, in the state of Andhra Pradesh, the Charminar—or Arc de Triomphe of the East—was built by Quli Qutub Shah in 1591 and is a fine example of architecture from the Qutub Shahi dynasty.

Page 75: Four-lion capital as seen on a pillar erected during the reign of Asoka (273–232 BC). The pillar itself is located in Sarnath, Varansi, in India.

Page 76 (top): Located in the Chandigarh Museum in Chandigarh, India, this Buddhist sculpture is a representation of the Bodhisattva Maitreya and is an example of works produced during the Gandharan period.

Page 76 (bottom): Carved between the third and fifth centuries, this Gandharan sculpture, known as *The Descent of the Buddha*, is now housed in the Victoria and Albert Museum in London, England.

Page 77 (top): Once a part of the Qutab Minar Mosque in Delhi, India, this pillar was first erected in 1368 during the reign of Emperor Firoz Tughlaq. It is believed to have originally been a part of a Hindu temple that was later turned into a mosque during or after the time of Islamic conquest in India.

Page 77 (bottom): Located in Sanchi, India, the Great Stupa is an important Buddhist monument that consists of burial mounds from the third century BC to the twelfth century AD.

Page 78: Located in Mahabalipuram, India, this carved boulder, designed in AD 640, is known as *Arjuna's Penance*, or *The Descent of the Ganges*, and is an example of Pallavan Hindu art of the period.

Page 79: The thirteenth-century medieval temple seen in this photo is known as the Kesava Temple and is located in Mysore, India.

Page 80: Located near the banks of the Bay of Bengal in India, the Surya Temple of Konarak is an example of medieval Indian architecture.

Page 84: This sixteenth-century painting is part of an edition of the Ramayana now located in the Freer Gallery of Art, part of the Smithsonian Institution, in Washington, D.C.

INDEX

A

Afghanistan, 21, 28, 44
ahimsa, 33, 70
Ajanta Caves, 22
Akbar, 28, 31, 72
Alexander the Great, 7, 75
All-India Muslim League, 32, 35
Amritsar, 33, 37
Andhras, 77
aqiqah ceremony, 60
Archean rocks, 11, 16
Aryabhata, 23
Aryans, 7, 20, 40, 66
asceticism, 67–68
Asoka, 17, 21–22, 44, 45, 76
Assam, 17
Aurangzeb, 29
ayurveda, 96

B

backgammon, 102
Baisakhi Festival, 55
Bangladesh, 11, 35, 37, 42
Bengal, 28–29, 41, 56
Bengali, 39, 42
Bentinck, Governor-General
        William, 31
Bhagavad Gita, 48
Bhutan, 11, 17
Bindusara, 21
bismillah ceremony, 60
Bombay/Mumbai, 29, 73, 82, 103
Brahma, 64–65
Brahman, 64, 66
Brahmin, 20, 64, 67–68, 85, 100
British East India Company, 29,
        31, 81
British raj, 32, 73, 88, 106, 109
brocade, 82
Buddha, 59, 65, 68–69, 75, 77, 100
Buddha Purnima, 59
Buddhism, 20–22, 63–64, 68, 86,
        100–101
Buddhists, 7, 100–101, 105

C

Calcutta, 29
caste, 20, 33, 55, 63–64, 72–73,
        100, 106
caste system, 20, 25, 69, 100–101
Chandragupta II, 22–23
Cheras, 23
chess, 102
Cholas, 23, 25
Christianity, 25, 63–64, 70, 73
Christians, 25, 63, 71–72
college, 108
Cyrus, 21

D

Delhi, 26, 31, 41
Delhi Sultanate, 26
democracy, 9, 32, 111
devadasis, 91
dharma, 47–48, 64–65, 100
dhimmi, 71
Dhritarashtra, 48
Diwali, 53
Dravidian languages, 42, 86
Dravidians, 45, 75, 77
Durga Puja, 56
Dussehra, 56
Dutch East India Company, 29
Dyer, General Reginald, 33

E

East Pakistan, 35, 37
edicts, 21, 44
Eightfold Path, 69
elephants, 17, 51, 53
Elizabeth I, Queen, 28
English (language), 39, 88

F

fables, 51, 85
festivals
    Baisakhi Festival, 55
    Buddha Purnima, 59
    Diwali, 56
    Durga Puja, 56
    Dussehra, 56
    Ganesh Chaturtui, 55
    Holi, 55
    Independence Day, 53
    Kumbh Mela, 53–54
    Naga Panchami, 55
    Pongol, 54
    Ramadan, 60
    Ram Lila, 56
    Republic Day, 53
    Sankranti, 54
    Shivrati, 55
    Vasant Panchami, 55
First War of Independence, 31
Four Noble Truths, 69

G

Gama, Vasco da, 28
Gandhi, Indira, 37
Gandhi, Mohandas Karamchand, 8,
        32–33, 35, 53, 63, 88, 100
Ganesh Chaturtui, 55
Ganga, 55
Ganges River, 11, 16, 55, 78–79
Gautama, Siddhartha, 20, 60, 68
Ghalib, Mirza Asadullah, 87
Goa, 28, 72
Golden Temple, 37
gopurams, 25
Green Revolution, 109
Gujarat, 26, 28, 29, 45, 111
Gupta Empire, 77
Guptas, 22

H

hajj, 71
Harappa, 19, 63, 75
Harappans, 44
hartal, 33
Himalayas, 7, 11–12, 13, 14,
        16, 17
Hindi, 39, 41–42, 45
Hinduism, 47, 59, 63, 66, 68, 70–71,
        86, 101
Hindus, 20, 28–29, 33, 35,
        41–42, 53, 55–56, 59–60,
        64–68, 72, 81, 94, 96–97,
        99–101, 111
Hindustani, 41, 87
Hitopadesa, 51
Holi, 55
Hyderabad, 30

I

incarnation, 47
Independence Day, 53
"Indian Mutiny," 31

Indian National Committee for Space Research (INCOSPAR), 110
Indian National Congress (INC), 32–33, 35
Indo-Aryan language, 39, 86
Indo-Gangetic Plain, 11, 13
Indra, 19–20, 67
Indus River, 11, 16, 19–20
Indus River Valley, 19, 75, 103
Integrated Rural Development Program (IRDP), 108–109
Islam, 28, 45, 63–64, 70–72, 101

J
Jainism, 20, 63–64, 70, 86
Jammu and Kashmir, 19
Jews, 25, 63, 71, 73
Jinnah, Mohammed Ali, 35
jizya tax, 28–29
Judaism, 70

K
Kalidasa, 23, 86
Kannada, 42
karma, 67
Kashmir, 19, 30, 51, 94, 97
kathakali, 91
Kerala, 42
khadi, 33
Khari Boli, 41
Khusrau, Amir, 87
Koran, 60, 70–71, 80–85, 97
Krishna, 47–48, 65, 82
Kshatriyas, 20
Kumbh Mela, 53–54

L
languages
    Bengali, 39, 42
    English, 39, 88
    Hindi, 39, 41–42, 45
    Hindustani, 41, 87
    Khari Boli, 41
    Marathi, 39, 45
    Nepali, 45
    Persian, 86–87, 105
    Punjabi, 39
    Sanskrit, 40–42, 45, 54, 57, 85–86, 105
    Tamil, 23, 39, 42

Telugu, 39, 42
    Urdu, 39, 41–42, 45, 87
lion, 17, 50–51

M
Madras (Chennai), 29
Mahabharata, 47–49, 85–86
maharajas, 30
Maharashtra, 56
Mahatma, 33, 35, 53
Mahavira, Vardhamana, 21
Malayalam, 42
Maldives, 13
mamluks, 26
Marathi, 39, 45
masalchi, 93
Maurya, Chandragupta, 21
Mauryan Empire, 21, 76
Mohenjo-Daro, 19–20
Mongols, 25
monk, 60, 82
monotheistic, 70
monsoon season, 13
Mount Everest, 12
Mughal Empire, 28–29, 72, 87, 105
Mughals, 28, 30, 83, 87
Muhammad, 60, 70–71
Mukteshvara Temple, 79
Muslims, 26, 28–29, 32–33, 35, 40–42, 45, 60–61, 63, 70–71, 79–81, 86–87, 94, 97–99, 101, 103, 111
MV Foundation, 107
Myanmar (Burma), 11
Mysore, 21, 29, 44

N
Naga, 55
Naga Panchami, 55
Nanak Guru, 70
Nanda dynasty, 21
Nandas, 21
Narmada River, 26
Natyashastra, 88
Navrati, 56
nawabs, 30
Nehru, Jawaharlal, 35, 37, 53, 88
Nepal, 17, 68
Nepali, 45
nikah, 61

nirvana, 69
Nobel Prize, 88
nuclear power, 110

O
opium, 29
outcastes, 20

P
Pakistan, 11, 13, 19, 35, 41–42, 45, 88, 102, 105, 111
Panchatantra, 51
Pandu, 48
Parabrahma, 64
Partition, 35, 41, 72, 88
peori, 80
Persia, 20–21, 72, 80
Persian, 86–87, 105
poachers, 17
Pongol, 54
primary education, 106
protest, 33
Punjab, 19, 26, 30, 35, 37, 41, 72, 87, 111
Punjabi, 39, 42
pyre, 31, 59

R
raja, 50
Rajasthan, 12, 26
Rama, 49, 56
Ramadan, 60
Ramayana, 47–49, 86–87
Ram Lila, 56
rani, 50
Raziya, 26
reincarnation, 67
rekha, 79
religions
    Buddhism, 20–22, 63–64, 68, 86, 100–101
    Christianity, 25, 63–64, 70, 73
    Hinduism, 47, 59, 63, 66, 68, 70–71, 86, 101
    Islam, 28, 45, 63–64, 70–72, 101
    Jainism, 20, 63–64, 70, 86
    Judaism, 70
    Sikhism, 63–64, 70
    Zoroastrianism, 72
Republic Day, 53

India: A Primary Source Cultural Guide

rhinoceros, 17
Rig Veda, 47, 57, 85
rudraksha, 96

S
sadhus, 54
Sankranti, 54
Sanskrit, 40–42, 45, 54, 57, 85–86, 105
Saraswati, 55, 65
saris, 82–83
sarod, 89
sati, 31
satyagraha, 33
script, 41–45
secondary school, 107–108
Sepoy Revolt, 31
sepoys, 31
sharia, 29
Shillong Plateau, 12
Shiva, 55, 64–66, 77, 90–91
Shivrati, 55
Shudras, 20
Sikhism, 63–64, 70
Sikhs, 30, 31, 45, 70, 72, 99
Singh, Ranjit, 30
Singh Rajah, 50
Sita, 49
sitar, 89

Slave Dynasty, 26
Somnath Temple, 26
spices, 93–94
Sri Lanka, 13, 42, 49, 68
states
    Assam, 17
    Bengal, 28–29, 41, 56
    Gujarat, 26, 28–29, 45, 111
    Hyderabad, 30
    Jammu and Kashmir, 19
    Kashmir, 30, 51, 94, 97
    Punjab, 19, 26, 30, 35, 37, 41, 72, 87, 111
    Rajasthan, 12
sultanate, 26, 28, 89
Surya Temple, 79

T
Tagore, Rabindranath, 88
Taj Mahal, 80–81
Tamil, 23, 39, 42
Tamil Nadu, 7, 42, 54–55, 57, 72, 90, 94
tandava, 91
tea, 29, 32
Telugu, 39, 42
Timur, 26
Tipu Sultan, 29
Todas, 102

tribes, 101
Tulsidas, 87

U
Urdu, 39, 41–42, 45, 87

V
Vaishyas, 20
Vajpayee, Atal Bihari, 37, 110
Valmiki, 49
Vasant Panchami, 55
Vedas, 19–20, 40, 64–65, 67, 85
vegetarians, 96–97
Victoria, Queen, 31
Vindhya Mountains, 11
Vishnu, 47–48, 55, 64–65, 87

W
West Pakistan, 35
White Revolution, 109

Y
yoga, 67–68, 90

Z
zamindars, 28
Zoroastrianism, 72

About the Author

Allison Stark Draper writes books for young readers on history and science. She lives in Stone Ridge, New York.

Editor: Joann Jovinelly; **Photo Editor:** Gillian Harper; **Cover Designer:** Tahara Hasan; **Designer:** Geri Giordano